# Buildings and Builders

# Buildings and Builders

*An Architectural History
of Boston University*

NANCY LURIE SALZMAN

With eighty-two photographs by Richard Cheek

Boston University

ISBN 0-87270-056-9

Boston University
Scholarly Publications
985 Commonwealth Avenue
Boston, Massachusetts 02215

Designed by David Ford

*To Esther Rhoads Houghton*
*and the late Professor Walter E. Houghton,*
*longtime friends and mentors,*
*who led me to explore the built environment*
*with a "Victorian Frame of Mind"*

# Contents

# Preface

This book is a descriptive guide to the buildings that have housed the facilities of Boston University since its incorporation on Beacon Hill by the Commonwealth of Massachusetts. In telling the story of these buildings, the book traces, in effect, the development of Boston University and the social, economic, and topographic context in which it grew. And, because virtually every style and type of local building is represented in these pages, the architectural history of the university reflects, in microcosm, the architectural history of Boston.

The "Builders" alluded to in the title are those persons who commissioned, designed, and constructed buildings—patrons like William Lindsay; architects like Vinal, Little, Cram, and Sert; and developers like Lawrence and Adams. The word also includes those visionaries who gave new life to old buildings, and created new buildings to meet old goals and aspirations—benefactors like Claflin, Rich, Sleeper, Mugar, and Danielsen, and presidents like Marsh, Case, and Silber.

If a book of this sort can be said to have a "plot," it may perhaps be found in the university's evolution from an inner-city institution, whose principal campus was the expanding city itself, to a self-contained community, closely associated with the surrounding cityscape but having a physical integrity of its own. An important subplot might well be the way in which the university managed to incorporate the heritage of the past into its visions of the future.

This book invites the reader to explore selected buildings of Boston University with increased awareness of the many layers of its past and the richness of its urban setting. Some are outstanding buildings of architectural importance; others are modest structures whose interest resides in their use of local tradition and materials.

Included here are a number of buildings which do not belong to the university, but whose proximity to the campus and whose visual significance afford a better understanding of the context in which the university took form. The Cottage Farm Historic District (Tour B) has a relatively high proportion of such buildings. This is because the university properties are widely dispersed among private dwellings of architectural and historical merit within one of America's first planned suburban developments.

The volume is divided into five walking tours, including a tour of some of the historic downtown buildings which served the university. Buildings are cross-referenced at the back by building type (e.g., apartment hotel), style (e.g., Gothic Revival), and architect. Technical terms which, in their initial appearance in the text are indicated by small capitals (e.g., NEO-CLASSICAL), are briefly defined in the Glossary of Architectural Terms.

# Acknowledgements

This book could not exist without the wise and tireless editing of Professor Keith N. Morgan, the unremitting support of Gerald J. Gross, the guidance of Patrick Gregory, the skills imparted by Professor Margaret Henderson Floyd, and the support and assistance of Helen B. Farquharson, Noreen O'Geara, Professor Gerald Powers, Ellie Reichlin of the Society for the Preservation of New England Antiquities, Nancy Shrock, Marcia Smilack, the staffs of the Boston University Special Collections of Mugar Memorial Library, Boston Public Library Fine Arts Department, Brookline Historical Commission, Harvard University Libraries, Wellesley College Art Library, Metropolitan District Commission and the authors, then and now, of chronicles documenting the never-ending story of the City of Boston. Finally, I would like to thank my husband, Edwin Salzman, for his unfailing encouragement.

N.L.S.

NOTE

Unless otherwise acknowledged, all the architectural photos in this book are by Richard Cheek.

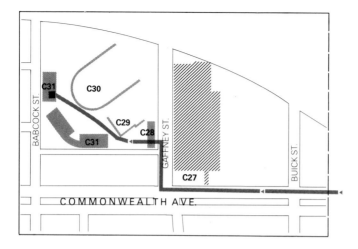
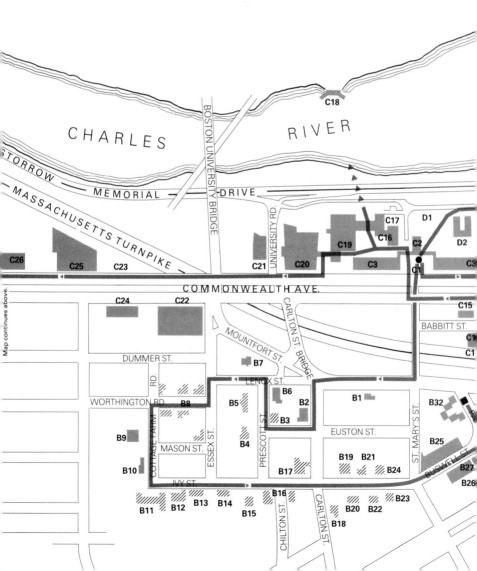

# The Charles River Campus and Environs

Indicating Walking Tours B, C, and D

Individual maps for Walking Tours A, B, C, and D will be found preceding those sections of the book

● Starting Point of Tours
■ Ending Points of Tours
■▶■ Walking Tours
University Properties
/// Privately Owned Properties

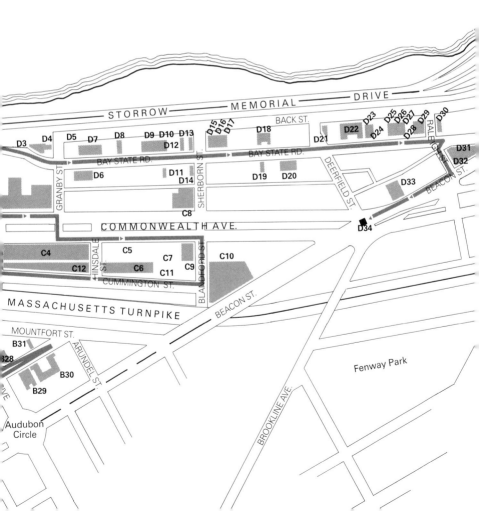

# Introduction

Since the university's establishment in Boston in 1869, succeeding generations of alumni have returned to a campus that differed radically from the scenes of their student days. Continual change seems to have characterized university policy. In response to its founders' hope that Boston University would truly become "Boston's University," the frequent shifts and transformations in the institution's physical setting reflected the dramatic dislocations of nineteenth-century Boston. And in spite—possibly because—of its migrations across the surface of the city, the university implanted deep roots in the cultural and intellectual life of Boston.

These founders—Lee Claflin, Isaac Rich, and Jacob Sleeper—represented the new, self-made mercantile generation of mid-nineteenth-century America. In the years following the Civil War, immigration and new technology altered the face of the nation. Nonetheless, American higher education still provided a narrow, middle-class training attuned to the traditions of an earlier age. The three Bostonians were among an avant-garde who recognized the necessity for a modern institution with high-quality graduate divisions. They looked across the river to Harvard, sleepily awaiting the great reforms of its twenty-first president, Charles Eliot, and declared that the time was ripe for a new urban university, one which would embody their own strong Methodist heritage of social equality in sex, race, and creed.

These three men were not newcomers to the field of education. For over thirty years they had collaborated in the establishment and administration of a number of educational institutions, including the Concord Biblical Institute in Concord, New Hampshire, whose transfer to Boston they arranged in 1867. The Institute later became the Boston University School of Theology, which shared its quarters in the new Wesleyan Building (A5) with the graduate School of Law.

In 1873, two recently combined medical institutions—the Female Medical College and the Massachusetts Homeopathic Hospital (A3)—became the Boston University Medical School. By 1875, Boston Univer-

sity had more graduate students in law, theology, and medicine than any
other American university, and a higher proportion of female students
than any similar institution. King's *1881 Handbook of Boston* stated
that "Boston University is distinguished by higher requirements for admission and the strictness with which it limits itself to purely collegiate
instruction."

The principles of institutional cooperation and economic opportun-
ism allowed the fledgling university to provide its students with facilities of high quality. Boston University students attended science classes
in the Back Bay premises of the recently founded Massachusetts Institute of Technology; and the first university-owned buildings on Beacon
Hill were renovated private homes and churches. Residents in flight
from the post–Civil War commercial expansion that had invaded the old
South End readily sold their properties to the university and migrated to
the tranquil settings recently made available by the Back Bay and New
South End landfill operations. This pattern was to repeat itself in the
post-World War I flight from the Back Bay to the suburbs, when the university enjoyed an extraordinary opportunity to acquire new properties
for its expanding needs. Thus from its beginnings, Boston University
played a significant role in the city's urban development, giving new life
and purpose to obsolete buildings and, in the process, reversing the decline of certain older neighborhoods.

Let us pause for a moment to survey the changing urban setting in
which Boston University was to make its home.

Colonial Boston was virtually an island, surrounded by the harbor and
a wide estuary of the Charles River, and connected to the mainland by
only a narrow neck of land. By 1800, post-Revolution prosperity stimulated the development of Federal-style townhouses flanking the prominent new State House on Beacon Hill. Designed by Charles Bulfinch,
this elegant monument reflected the influence of the English architect
Robert Adam, whose NEO-CLASSICAL buildings based upon classical OR-
DERS Bulfinch had studied at first hand in England. These Federal-style
buildings featured embellishments of wood or stone trim and delicate
ironwork; short flights of steps led to front doorways crowned with el-
liptical, leaded-glass fanlights; windows became proportionally smaller
at successive floors; and sometimes the uppermost stories were joined
within PILASTER columns and a roof balustrade. This architectural vocabulary would reappear a century later along Bay State Road (Tour D) in
the form of FEDERAL REVIVAL buildings.

Meanwhile, the GREEK REVIVAL townhouses of the 1830s reiterated the

*Brookline Fort, center left, located near the mouth of the Charles River, is the site of the present Boston University Bridge. From an 1806 map of Revolutionary Boston. (Society for the Preservation of New England Antiquities)*

simplicity of the Federal ornament, but with heavier classical proportions. Here, solid granite post-and-LINTEL PORTICOS with rectangular sidelights heralded an allegiance to the egalitarian principles of Greek (i.e., American) democracy.

In 1821, the Boston and Roxbury Mill Corporation completed a mill dam fifty feet wide and one and a half miles long across the back bay of the Charles River to Sewall's Point in Brookline. Although the purpose of the dam was to provide water power for small mills, this 6½-cent-toll roadway attracted a few wealthy summer residents, among them David Sears. In 1850, textile magnates Amos and William Lawrence purchased 200 acres adjoining Sears at Cottage Farm in Brookline.

Influenced by the popular tastemaker, Andrew Jackson Downing, the Lawrence family commissioned picturesque EARLY GOTHIC REVIVAL–style cottages for themselves and their friends. These stone or brick cottages with their steep, cross-gable roofs and chapel-like entries nestled within a private park landscape. Later mansions adopted the classical ITALIANATE AND SECOND EMPIRE styles, sometimes in combination with Gothic details. The largest of these, the Sears-Talbot house (B9), is a Boston University faculty residence, while a small cottage houses an academic department (B1). Such a rural setting became a year-round residential option with the opening of the Boston and Worcester Railroad's Cottage Farm station in 1855.

By 1849, the stagnant waters behind the mill dam from Charles Street to the crossdam at Gravelly Point (the corner of Massachusetts and Commonwealth Avenues) had become such a nuisance that the city ordered the owners to fill in this "back" bay. The filling, which commenced in 1857, coincided with the increasing demand for residential housing, away from the hustle-and-bustle of downtown Boston, and the new 25-foot-wide lots were eagerly snatched up.

The landfill project provided the opportunity for architect Arthur Gilman to introduce elements of the new French Second Empire urban planning that had successfully transformed Paris from a cluster of labyrinthine streets and alleyways to a spaciously conceived national capital. Work proceeded on a grand Public Garden and a rational street grid. The centerpiece, Commonwealth Avenue, cut a wide, 100-foot swath of park flanked by carriageways and intersected regularly by cross streets alphabetically evoking British history. Symmetrical FACADES of oversized windows with prominent enframements lined the streets of classical Italianate and Second Empire–style brownstone townhouses.

Churches (A9, 10) and cultural institutions followed their members into the new Back Bay. At the corner of Berkeley and Newbury Streets,

*Copley Square, with the foundation of the Boston Public Library in the foreground. This view is from the old Harvard Medical School, rededicated in 1908 as Boston University. (The Bostonian Society)*

architect William Preston (A3, 9) designed a splendid Museum of Natural History, erected in 1862 and followed, two years later, by Rogers Hall, a companion structure for Massachusetts Institute of Technology. Boston University students would soon be utilizing Rogers Hall for their own science classes and, as departments and enrollment expanded, the university purchased and readapted a number of neighboring townhouses.

At Dartmouth Street, the grid clashed with the diagonal route of the railroad tracks, isolating a large, triangular plot. Unsuitable for houses, it became a civic center, named for John Copley, the artist-owner of the site of the first brick townhouse (A1) on Beacon Hill. In the early 1870s, Copley Square became an even more splendid cultural focus. Along the south side, on the present site of the Copley Plaza Hotel (1912), rose a Museum of Fine Arts (1871–74) designed by Sturgis and Bingham in a panel brick and TERRA-COTTA Ruskinian Gothic style. Opposite were two great stone churches: at the northwest corner, the HIGH VICTORIAN GOTHIC New Old South Church (1874) by Cummings and Sears and, along the eastern edge, the innovative ROMANESQUE REVIVAL Trinity Church (1872–77) by Henry Hobson Richardson. Trinity Church represented a conscious collaboration between the architect and artisans to create a unified decorative scheme. These civic monuments influenced design motifs in a wide array of townhouses and mansion styles along neighboring streets.

At the far western end of Copley Square at Exeter Street, Harvard University commissioned Ware and Van Brunt, the architects of its Civil War Memorial Hall, to design spacious buildings for its medical school. (One building [A11] would be rededicated in 1908 as the new home of Boston University.) Six years later, in 1888, the final jewel was set into

*Bay State Road and Boston University's Charles River Campus will rise on the landfill between Brighton (now Commonwealth) Avenue and the Harbor Commissioners' Line at the top of the map. (From* Atlas of Suffolk County, *1874)*

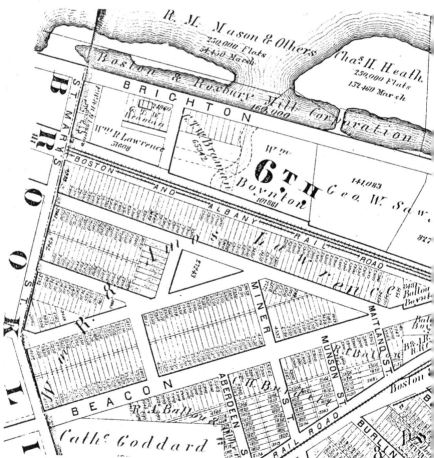

the crown, on the west side of Copley Square alongside the Harvard Medical School: the landmark CLASSICAL REVIVAL-style Boston Public Library, a "palace for the people," designed by the firm of McKim, Mead and White.

The topography of Boston underwent a second, radical alteration in the hands of Frederick Law Olmsted, the nation's first major landscape architect and the designer of New York's Central Park. Olmsted had developed, by necessity, into an adroit administrator and accomplished engineer. He convinced Boston officials that they could in one fell swoop turn the Fens—the foul, sewage-filled marshes of the Muddy River at the west end of Commonwealth Avenue—into a part of a "sanitary . . . emerald necklace" of water parks and, in the bargain, create a new tax base with the adjacent filled land to pay for the project.

Olmsted shifted the axis of Commonwealth Avenue northwest from this park along Brighton Avenue, renaming it as Commonwealth. Again,

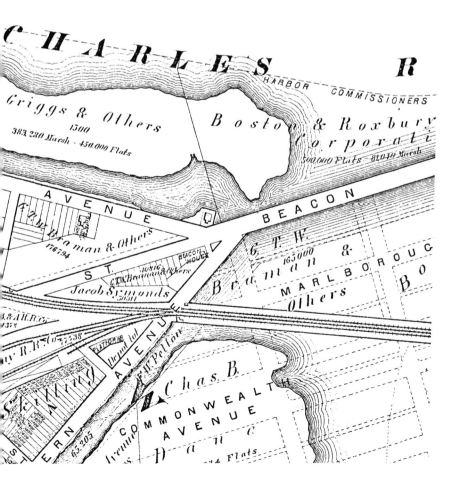

as at Copley Square, the street pattern conflicted with the railroad lines, creating another triangular space, briefly named Governor's and, now, Kenmore Square. South of the railroad, Olmsted Associates had, by 1887, extended Beacon Street into Brookline as a broad, 160-foot-wide boulevard down the middle of which trolley lines transported commuters to new, low-priced SPECULATOR-built housing. These rowhouses changed hands repeatedly for almost a century until the late 1970s when purchased by Boston University to form the South Campus.

North of the railroad tracks, the potential use for nearly 750,000 square feet of Charles River tidal flats was recognized by John Quincy Adams, Jr., and his father, Charles Francis Adams, Jr., President of the Riverbank Improvement Corp. The Adamses constructed a granite wall, still intact as the south side of Storrow Drive, along a line in the river drawn by the Harbor Commissioners. They dumped fill to create Bay State Road and enacted a strict set of building guidelines, which were to assure and protect the high quality and fine appearance of the neighborhood.

West Back Bay builders N. Henry Chadwick and George Wheatland, along with architects Arthur Vinal and Edmund Wheelright, leapfrogged the Fens/park boundary and raced along the elegant Bay State Road and onto the smaller streets laid out south of the railroad on the Lawrence brothers' Boston estates, east of their Cottage Farm properties. In less than fifteen years, three- and four-story red-brick rowhouses, townhouses, and mansions almost completely covered the area, recreating a revival of Federal Beacon Hill. In 1905, *The Brickbuilder* remarked that—

> to match exactly the conditions of old Beacon Street, even with its sea wall and squalid rear alley, was their highest ambition. "Colonial" expression was regarded as of paramount importance.

Flushed with success, Adams invested his Bay State Road profits into another 1,563,092 square feet between Commonwealth Avenue and the railroad west of the Cottage Farm bridge. To the north of Adams' new property lay Beacon Park, 2,784,756 square feet of pleasure ground and carriage track owned by Eban Jordan. Adams' purchase seemed a prudent move, since new mansions were being erected alongside the Lawrence family's Cottage Farm residences just south of Adams' land. One of these houses, the Curtis residence, now serves as administrative offices for Boston University (B6); another is the president's mansion (B2).

Curiously, Commonwealth Avenue west of Kenmore Square remained virtually unbuilt. In 1902, Arthur Vinal filed building permits for houses clustered on circular CUL-DE-SACS opening off Commonwealth Avenue

*855 Commonwealth Avenue, the present School for the Arts, was originally designed as showrooms for Buick automobiles. (From* The American Architect and Building News, *vol. XXI, no. 2357, 1921)*

between Blandford and Hinsdale Streets. Alongside these proposed house lots, the distinguished Congregation Adath Israel build an imposing marble temple, centering it between the fashionable and ever-expanding Back Bay and Cottage Farm/Brookline neighborhoods. These neighborhoods, however, failed to grow. The Temple, now Morse Hall (C9), was left to stand alone on the vacant avenue like a great white-marble elephant.

The second decade of the twentieth century found the map of west Boston in uneasy equilibrium. On the south end of Jordan's Beacon Park stood a new railroad roundhouse. Adams evidently abandoned plans for a housing development for his Cottage Farm land and converted it into the Allston Golf Club. On Bay State Road, a few small-scale speculator houses had filled in at #110–118 (D20) and three apartment houses (including D2) rose west of Granby Street. The Lawrence Trust released its protected corner lots (B27, 28) at Park Drive and Ivy (now Buswell) Street for apartment, not mansion construction; the northwest corner remained unsold until 1913, and then became retail shops, not housing.

A brash newcomer, the automobile showroom, had now begun to take over Commonwealth Avenue. It adopted the revival styles of the neighborhood, COLONIAL, TUDOR, and Gothic, but adapted them to its own peculiar ends. The large commercial palaces soon formed a solid mile-long wall stretching from Kenmore Square into Brighton. On back streets, such as Cummington, two-story garages and repair shops (C6, 7, 10–14) in a concrete and brick industrial mode replaced neighborhood stables and rendered the area undesirable for residential housing. Flanked on one side by railroad lines, western Commonwealth Avenue was selected as appropriate for the Massachusetts Armory (C27) and manufacturing plants. Some of these new factories took their coloration from the castle-like Tudor-style Armory by utilizing red brick with limestone bands, tower-pavilions, and roof-top CRENELLATION. In recent years, most of these commercial and industrial buildings have been adapted to new uses within the university.

In the mid 1920s, a number of large, luxury apartment hotels (B30, D22, 31) filled the remaining unbuilt lots along Bay State Road. But by the 1930s, fashions and land use had again changed. Back Bay townhouse residents, flocking to the suburbs, sold their properties for reuse as professional offices, small schools, apartments, and boarding houses. In 1936, the opening of the Lahey Clinic at Sherborn Street (C8) turned Bay State Road into an enclave of doctors' offices. Cottage Farm, however, remained exclusive and residential. Its last open spaces were filled with Tudor, GEORGIAN, and Federal Revival homes.

The collapse of a century-long residential townhouse boom left in its wake a large unbuilt tract west of Granby Street between the river and Boston's finest and grandest boulevard, Commonwealth Avenue. Boston University trustees purchased this land in 1920 and, soon after, were able to change the residential height restrictions from 80 to 155 feet. President Marsh wrote in 1927, "By erecting some of the buildings to this height, it would be possible to house all the departments with twice our present enrollment." The trustees commissioned the foremost LATE-GOTHIC-REVIVAL architect, Ralph Adams Cram, to create and plan for a riverside campus of quiet quadrangles dominated by a chapel. Nothing was built for two decades; but as Professor Ault wrote in his history of the university:

> . . . in the meantime Presidents could dream. President Murlin clipped a picture of the 680' high "Cathedral" which the University of Pittsburgh had erected and pinned to it this note, "This is my dream for Boston University except we cannot go so high in Boston."

And in the meantime, too, the trustees had filled in 100 feet out over the tidal flats to form a riverside terrace only to have it abruptly seized by the Metropolitan District Commission for Storrow Embankment Park in 1929–31 (and, in 1951, for Storrow Drive). Suddenly, in 1939, the

# The Myles Standish

BAY STATE ROAD AND BEACON STREET

BOSTON

BOSTON'S Newest Housekeeping Apartment Hotel is available for occupancy.

The Myles Standish combines, as far as is possible, the advantages of an hotel, an apartment house and a private home.

✿

Full hotel service will be supplied; maid service, valet service, dining room service and telephone switchboard service. In addition to the complete advantages of the most modern hotel, every apartment is fully equipped for housekeeping, with the best type of efficiency kitchen and dining alcove. Continuous refrigeration is supplied from a cold storage plant, without extra charge, and the newest type tubular boilers, fired with oil, insure all the hot water and heat desirable.

IT would be hard to excel the location of the Myles Standish for a city home. It is central in the full sense of the word.

The corner of Bay State Road and Beacon Street is the heart of the Back Bay district, a section known the world over as the fashionable part of Boston. The Kenmore entrance of the subway at Governor Square is within a minute's walking distance, and a large garage, (while completely hidden from view,) is equally convenient. The business section of Boston is about twenty minutes walk along Beacon Street.

✿

From the higher floors on the Bay State Road side the view of the Charles River and Cambridge is splendid. At night, the silver ribbon of the river with its many bridges and myriad lights is rivalled only by some Venetian scene.

✿

The Front - Bay State Road Side

A 1925 promotional announcement for the Myles Standish Apartment Hotel, now a Boston University dormitory. (Society for the Preservation of New England Antiquities)

*A representation of President Murlin's "dream" campus, from a 1925 university fund-raising brochure. (Boston University Special Collections)*

university's lease in M.I.T.'s Walker Building on Newbury Street was terminated and the building demolished for the erection of the New England Life block. To rehouse the School of Management, the trustees hurriedly erected Charles Hayden Memorial Hall (C3).

After World War II, the enormous increase in enrollment forced the university to implement the Cram master plan. Only the south side of the quadrangles was constructed, pressing against the now-busy streetcar lines along Commonwealth Avenue. The initial building, the College of Liberal Arts, was still unfinished when the semester opened in September 1947. Professor Ault writes further:

> Professor Malcolm Agnew of the Classics Department wrote a poem in Latin which reads in part: "Now we have stayed here long enough, Here the Square (Copley), racked by its city winds, has dirtied us learned men long enough."

Already-converted townhouses along Bay State Road provided additional dormitory and administrative space. For official resident and academic purposes, the university acquired some Cottage Farm mansions in the 1960s. Consistent with a now century-old policy of adaptive reuse, the growing university obtained needed space in nearby auto showrooms and factories through remodeling rather than demolition and new construction. This policy preserved intact a visual record of the historic development of the area, while new infill on vacant lots added a Contemporary-style link with its architectural evolution. In the early 1960s, José Luis Sert placed his glass and concrete high-rise structures on a quad-like site behind the Cram complex, thus restoring the original concept of protected inner courtyards, masked from the confusion of the city.

The late seventies found the university shaping its plans to the desires of the community. It converted many Bay State Road dormitories to administrative offices or rentals and moved the students to the speculator rowhouses and apartment buildings south of the railroad. These rowhouses had changed hands repeatedly over the past century, reaching a low point in the 1930s when neighbors in the fashionable Cottage Farm petitioned the City of Boston to rename Ivy as Buswell Street and remove its colorful but unsavory reputation from their doorsteps.

As we enter the 1980s, Boston University has stabilized the area with renovations, landscaping, and added security. The university has now turned its attention to Kenmore Square with its heritage of recycled auto showrooms, apartment hotels, and townhouses, which was until recently a jungle of fast-food shops, boutiques, and office services. The revitalization of this area (D34) which is under way should provide an attractive focal point for the westernmost end of Boston's Back Bay, while ensuring the expanded architectural integrity of the university.

*Boston University's Charles River Campus forms a western boundary of the city of Boston. (Boston University Photo Services)*

*Tour A*

# The Historic and Downtown Campuses

## *Tour A* **The Historic and Downtown Campuses**

A1  37½ Beacon Street
A2  71–73 Summer Street
A3  18–20 Beacon Street
A4  80 East Concord Street,
    School of Medicine
A5  36 Bromfield Street
A6  Tremont and East

    Newton Streets,
    Franklin Square House
A7  70–72 Mt. Vernon
    Street
A8  27 Chestnut Street
A9  12 Somerset Street.
    Demolished.

A10  11 Ashburton Place.
     Demolished.
A11  688 Boylston Street
A12  264 Huntington
     Avenue, Boston
     University Theatre

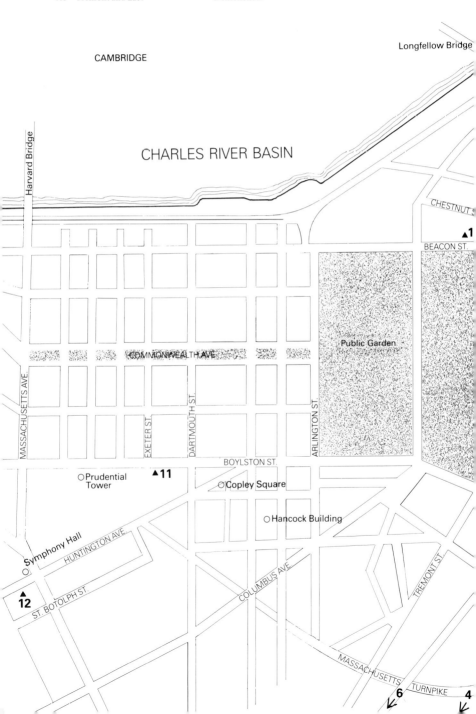

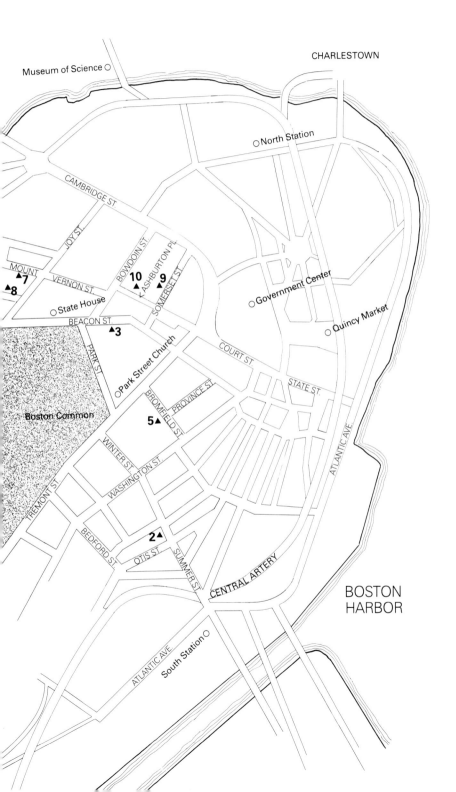

On May 26, 1869, three self-made businessmen created the legal entity which was to inherit the fruits of their lifelong labors, an institution of higher learning. Deeply religious and socially conscious Methodist lay leaders, they hoped to "enrich other lives with what had been denied their own." Their newest philanthropy they named Boston University in honor of the opportunities and riches the metropolis had bestowed upon them. Their lives illustrate the forces which fueled the explosive growth of mid-nineteenth-century Boston.

Lee Claflin (1791–1871) was the prime mover in the founding of Boston University; he made it his heir and applied for its charter. Extremely poor as a child, he apprenticed to a New Hampshire farmer at the age of five, and with legendary Yankee zeal, ultimately established the first shoe factory in New England. This burgeoning enterprise provided him with the wealth to pursue his highly disciplined philanthropic habits. (Claflin faithfully recorded his contributions in a diary at the end of each Sabbath.) His eldest son, William Claflin, following his father's example, assisted in the establishment of the New England Conservatory of Music (A6) and was the first trustee of Wellesley College. As Governor of Massachusetts, William Claflin signed the incorporation charter for Boston University.

The petition for the university's incorporation was signed at 37½ Beacon Street (A1), the home of Isaac Rich (1801–1872).

*Lee Claflin. (Boston University Special Collections)*

## A1/37½ Beacon Street

Phillips House, Charles Bulfinch, 1804; c. 1850 altered; 1864, home of Isaac Rich, founder. Private.*

The first Federal-style brick house on this site was designed by the noted architect Charles Bulfinch and built in 1804 for John Phillips, who, after twenty-five years in the state legislature, became the first mayor of the City of Boston in 1822. It was here that his son, the great abolitionist Wendell Phillips, was born. After John Phillips' death in 1825, the house be-

* Information in building headings is given in the following sequence: address, name or description of building, architect, date of construction; date and nature of remodeling, architect; date and nature of subsequent use. Privately-owned properties are so indicated. (Names and dates are included when available.)

came the home of Lieutenant Governor Thomas Winthrop, descendant of the first governor of Massachusetts, and his wife, a granddaughter of Governor Bowdoin. During the mid-century, the building was remodeled in the Italianate style, with large windows replacing the five-bay front, and with a new entryway on Walnut Street.

The owner of this mansion in 1864 was Isaac Rich, one of the founders of Boston University. As a boy, Rich had supported his widowed mother and family by selling oysters from a pushcart outside Boston's Quincy Market. By 1869, his fishing fleet dominated the import and export of fish throughout New England, and from the profits of this industry, he had acquired extensive real estate in the City of Boston. Following the death of his wife and only child, Rich "hoped to fulfill their promise through philanthropy" and, on his own death in 1872, bequeathed to Boston University an es-

*Phillips House, on left, circa 1804, home of Boston University founder Isaac Rich. (From* Winsor's Memorial History of Boston*)*

*Jacob Sleeper. (Boston University Special Collections)*

*Isaac Rich. (Boston University Special Collections)*

tate valued at $1,200,000. (Within the year, the Great Fire of 1872 leveled 776 buildings on 65 acres of the central business district, reducing by one half the value of this inheritance.)

The original Bulfinch design on this site set a pattern for many of the buildings on Beacon Hill—and the style enjoyed a revival almost a century later throughout the newly developed Back Bay area. Thus it might be said that Boston University's founder's home on Beacon Hill was to inspire the design of an important segment of the present campus—the buildings alongside Bay State Road (Tour D).

The third benefactor, Jacob Sleeper (1802–1889) grew wealthy from another of Boston's chief industries. Utilizing the output of the thriving New England textile mills, pioneered by the Lawrence brothers (Tour B), Sleeper built up a clothing manufacturing business. From this, he amassed an estate of $400,000 which

he promised to the new university, "provided it will have a Methodist tenor."

## A2/71–73 Summer Street

Cast-iron commercial building, 1873, gift of Jacob Sleeper, founder, to Boston University. Private.

Sleeper's bequest to the new university included 71–73 Summer Street, one of the few cast-iron buildings now surviving in Boston. Built in 1873, immediately following the Great Fire, its lavish detail reflects Sleeper's pride in the rebirth of his city. Constructed of precast iron elements chosen from building catalogues, the structure was erected quickly. The six-story, four-bay building combines traditional robust, rounded ITALIAN RENAISSANCE forms with a new, NEO-GREC emphasis upon flat, incised, geometric orna-

*71–73 Summer Street.*

*The first home of the College of Liberal Arts, 18–20 Beacon Street, from a photo taken in the 1870s. (Courtesy Boston University Special Collections)*

ment. The middle floors feature FLUTED half columns which separate the arched windows and support a MODILLION CORNICE. On the top two floors, STRIATED pilasters separate rectangular windows and support a DENTIL cornice with paired BRACKET on each side. The two ground floors have

been totally modernized with no concern for the upper facade.

### A3/18–20 Beacon Street

Site of two c. 1820 townhouses; 1884, the Claflin Building, William G. Preston; School of Religious Education and Social Service; 1873, first home of the Boston University College of Liberal Arts. Private.

*18 Beacon Street. (Society for the Preservation of New England Antiquities)*

The fledgling university was located on stylish Beacon Hill, in a pair of Greek Revival–style townhouses diagonally across from the State House. Number 20 was demolished for the Claflin Building, and the portico of #18 was modified. However, #16 still flanks the site, with its smooth facade, flush windows with stone sills, modillion cornices and, on the left, the remaining half of a stone DORIC portico or porch. On the site of #18–20, Professor Alexander Graham Bell taught vocal physiology, "the mechanism of speech" to Boston University students.

The university soon outgrew these quarters and, in 1882, commissioned W. G. Preston to remodel a nearby church into a new home for the College of Liberal Arts. The same architect then cleared the site at #20 and erected the present structure to serve as the School for Religious Education and Social Service, reorganized into the School of Social Work in 1940.

The eclectic collection of stylistic motifs is controlled by a bold, three-BAY symmetrical composition. Heavy RUSTICATED columns of QUARRY-FACED stone frame the ground floor doorway and commercial plate glass windows. In the SPANDRELS between the arches, the terra-cotta portrait plaques of the artists Albrect Dürer and Anton van Dijk (Anthony van Dyke) separate the three window arches, which terminate in paired columns. On the upper floors, smooth limestone forms a background for decorative terra-cotta bands which define each level, the first of which features the "B.U." monogram.

Vertical treatment is playful and original. The side sections at levels three to five contain unusual bay windows, angled out from the wall and set in copper sheathing embossed with typical QUEEN ANNE REVIVAL patterns: ROSETTES and chrysanthemums. The roofline is richly ornamented by a pair of triangular PEDIMENTS, a balustrade, and, on the west facade, an elaborate chimney/window composition.

## A4/80 East Concord Street

Massachusetts Homeopathic Hospital, William Emerson, 1871/1884/1892; 1873, Boston University School of Medicine.

In 1855, eight physicians, expelled from the Massachusetts Medical Society for the practice of homeopathic medicine, banded together to found their own hospital.

In 1871, the New England Female Medical College commissioned a medical school building. Work on the structure was begun near Boston City Hospital, but by the following spring, the college was bankrupt.

At this point, Dr. Israel Talbot (1829–1899), a staff member of the Homeopathic Hospital on Burroughs Street, who three years earlier had participated in the founding of Boston University, intervened. In October 1872 the Homeopaths assumed the debt of $42,000 for the medical school building. Aware that his hospital possessed a state charter enabling it to establish a medical school, Talbot brought together the Homeopaths with their charter, the Female Medical College with its faculty and new facility, and Boston University—thereby creating the Boston University School of Medicine. The initial class, one third of it women, was the first in the country to train under a graded course of instruction.

Built in three stages, the building is

*80 East Concord Street. On left, Female Medical College classroom building; on right, Massachusetts Homeopathic Hospital. (From* King's Handbook of Boston*)*

one of Boston's liveliest and most eclectic architectural creations. The 1876 center section trumpets High Victorian Gothic POLYCHROMY and reverberates with the sort of decorative symbolism endorsed by the English art philosopher John Ruskin. The rhythmic movement and massing of horizontal and vertical spaces create a sense of bold energy and playfulness. Most notable is the massive arch with its moon gate, horseshoe-shaped arch, squat piers and, on the tower, the JERKINHEAD dormer enclosing a triangular window.

As the institution flourished, Queen Anne–style wings were added in 1884 and 1892. Somewhat tamer in their impact, they continue the theme of large gable entry porches and decorative brick. A slender central stair-tower and a large octagonal bay with

tower along with the side piers and chimneys provide vertical thrust.

## A5/36 Bromfield Street

The Wesleyan Building, Hammat Billings, 1870; home of Boston University School of Theology (1870) and School of Law (1872). Private.

Theological studies were a particular concern of the founders of the new university. These men already served as trustees of the Concord, New Hampshire, Biblical Institute, founded in 1833 in Newbury, Vermont, where Claflin was president, Rich vice president, and Sleeper treasurer. In 1867, Claflin arranged for the Institute's move from the country to the Wesleyan Building in Boston where it shared quarters with a variety of Methodist enterprises, among them *Zion's Herald* and the Women's Christian Temperance Union (WCTU). Two years later, in 1869, the Concord Biblical Institute was incor-

25

*36 Bromfield Street. (From King's Hand-
book of Boston)*

porated as the new Boston University
Graduate School of Theology. The
Law School also found quarters here
from 1872 to 1884. As with the "modern" medical school, the university
tightened the law curriculum, requir-
ing three years of study, an unusually
high standard for the times.

The Wesleyan Building rested on
the site of the seventeenth-century
home of Edward Bromfield, a prominent merchant. As this area between
Washington and Tremont Streets in
the Old South End changed and gave
way to commerce, Bromfield's home
was converted into a famous stage-
coach stop, the Indian Queen Tavern.
In 1835, Claflin, Rich, and Sleeper all
became active in the 1809 Methodist
Chapel next door at #32 and, in 1849,
financed its remodeling. The chapel
and tavern were uneasy neighbors until 1870 when church trustees purchased and demolished the tavern to

make way for this imposing, four-story, seven-bay, granite Methodist headquarters.

The Wesleyan Building, a major Boston Historic Landmark, is one of the finest intact examples of the designs of Hammatt Billings (1818–1875) to survive the Fire of 1872. Here is a high-style design from an architect whose career spanned almost a century of fashions: from his apprenticeship with Asher Benjamin (author of popular Builder's Guides in the Federal style) and with Amni B. Young (designer of the Greek Revival Boston Custom House) to his own Wesleyan Building and Wellesley College, built in Second Empire style in 1876. Billings combined the new Neo-Grec ornament of flat, stylized, incised design

with French Second Empire–style MANSARD roofs, prominent dormers, and PAVILION composition. The interior is in poor condition, although most of the original oak woodwork, glass-paned doors, and early cast-iron radiators remain. Today, the Methodist Church no longer owns the building.

### A6/Franklin Square House

Tremont and East Newton Streets, built as St. James Hotel, Maturin M. Ballou, 1867; 1882, New England Conservatory of Music and Boston University School of Music; housing for elderly. Private.

From its beginnings, Boston University allied its fledgling schools with established institutions. The Boston University College of Music formed a unique relationship with the New England Conservatory of Music. Governor William Claflin, son of founder Lee Claflin, had expressed his philanthropic concerns by founding the con-

---

*The luxurious St. James Hotel, built in 1867, was meant to set the tone for the new South End. In 1882 it became the home of the New England Conservatory of Music. (Boston University Special Collections)*

servatory in 1867. Its director, Dr. Eban Tourjee, was none other than the music director of the Claflins' Bromfield Street Methodist Church.

The conservatory was the first advanced institution of its kind in America, accepting only graduate-level students with degrees from other "musical colleges and conservatories." In 1872, Boston University similarly accepted "advanced pupils with an eye to productive musicianship," who shared the dean, faculty, and facilities, and were awarded a joint degree.

In 1882, the conservatory moved with its Boston University component from the Bromfield Street Music Hall (now remodeled as the Orpheum Theater) to the former St. James Hotel in the South End. Dominating Franklin Square, the grandiose brick-and-stone facade in Second Empire style emulated the new Boston City Hall (1861–65) by Bryant and Gilman, architects of the first Boston City Hospital (A4). The building was the largest family hotel in the city and the most expensively furnished.

The six-and-a-half stories and twenty-one bays create a rhythmic effect with the long rows of identical windows accented with strong segmental limestone HOODS. Center and end pavilions and heavy stone QUOINS provide vertical emphasis. In the central bay of modified PALLADIAN windows, a massive entrance portico of double columns supports a ceremonial balcony with urn-shaped balustrade. A dramatic, dark, mansard roof, punctuated by arched dormers and convex, curving towers firmly crowns the massive facade.

In 1901, the New England Conservatory moved to its present quarters next to the Boston University Theatre

across from Symphony Hall and the now-lost Opera House. In 1980, the great building on Franklin Square was renovated as subsidized housing for the elderly.

## A7/70–72 Mt. Vernon Street

John E. and Nathaniel Thayer double mansion, Richard Upjohn? 1847; 1884–1950, Boston University School of Theology; 1965–70, condominiums, Bullerjahn Associates.

The second home of the School of Theology, a double mansion, was renamed Warren Hall to honor the first president of the university. This Beacon Hill landmark imitates an Italian Renaissance palace, a mode popularized in the exclusive clubs along Pall Mall in London and in the 1847 Boston Athenaeum.

A low wall with intact cast-iron railing separates the strongly organized building mass from the sidewalk. The side pavilions are handled forcefully through the use of heavy, rusticated stone quoins, oversized arched doorways surmounted by a stone balustrade, heavy bracketed window hoods, and a projecting cornice crowning the fourth floor.

All windows are flush within the stone facade but vary in size, SASH, and treatment at each level. At the second floor, the present Federal Revival–style metal frames replaced the former late-nineteenth-century TRANSOM windows, themselves replacements. The top-story windows double in number to form an arcade but recede visually through reduction in size.

Attached to the rear and facing

*70–72 Mount Vernon Street.*

28

Chestnut Street is the 1916 Robinson Chapel (A8). When the School of Theology moved to the Charles River Campus, both buildings were sold, and they have been converted to condominiums.

---

*27 Chestnut Street.*

## A8/27 Chestnut Street

Robinson Chapel, School of Theology, Bellows and Aldrich, 1916; 1964, condominiums, Bullerjahn Associates. Private.

In 1916, the School of Theology on Mt. Vernon Street (A7) added a chapel extension attached at the rear, but 22 feet lower and facing onto Chestnut

*12 Somerset Street. (Boston University Special Collections)*

Street. The architects chose a chaste but correct Late Gothic Revival form, a style so popular in university building throughout America that it became known as COLLEGIATE GOTHIC.

In spite of its mass, the 70-foot-high chapel harmonizes with its neighboring townhouses through sensitive proportioning. Verticality is achieved on the street facade by the use of heavy stone BUTTRESSES that separate multistory pointed arches, within which rested stained-glass windows. This stained glass was removed in 1950 and incorporated into the design of the new Marsh Chapel (C2) and School of Theology (C3) on the Charles River Campus. The lower floors featured

narrow, paired, pointed arches also set with stained glass, since removed. The exterior ornamentation is simple, with some TREFOILS inset in stone.

The interior contained richly carved oak screens, canopies, communion rails, and a pulpit. Even the balcony railing was elaborate. The original heavy oak doors with their dramatic hand-wrought hinges of iron still remain.

### A9/12 Somerset Street

First Baptist Church, 1853; 1883, remodeled into Jacob Sleeper Hall, College of Liberal Arts and School of All Sciences (Graduate School), William G. Preston. Demolished.

By 1882, the young College of Liberal Arts had outgrown its quarters at 18–20 Beacon Street. Nearby, the Univer-

*The reading room fireplace at 12 Somerset Street. (Boston University Special Collections)*

sity found a vacant 1853 Baptist Church whose congregation, responding to commercial pressures in central Boston, had joined the flight to the newly fashionable Back Bay. At a cost of $65,000 to the school, W. G. Preston created a 10,000-square-foot interior space. Limited by the church proportions and window openings, he refaced the exterior with red pressed brick and removed "the most prominent (219-foot) spire in Boston."

The symmetrical, three-bay facade featured tall windows with QUARRY-GLASS transoms, separated into groups of four by vertical pilasters. Ornamentation focused upon the central bay with a segmental arched doorway, a

bay window at the second level, and a modest triangular pediment at the roofline. Horizontal bands of limestone connected the window elements.

The interior reflected the latest English Queen Anne Revival style, the architect Preston's forte. In the reading room, he created a full-length fireplace composition with various shapes of molded brick, terra-cotta panels, and Minton tiles. The wooden benches alongside the chimney breast displayed curved arms, embellished with a sunburst carving. Alumni nostalgically remember the building for its "cavernous basement room" and the catacombs which connected it with the two adjacent houses occupied by the School of Law.

One hundred years later, all that marks the site is a parking lot.

### A10/11 Ashburton Place

Mt. Vernon Church, 1842; 1884, remodeled into Isaac Rich Hall, School of Law, William G. Preston; demolished.

Within three years of its founding, Boston University established a Law School in the Wesleyan Building (A5). For the next two decades, the school moved about on Beacon Hill. From 1886 to 1895, it was strategically located near the State House and the Pemberton Square site for the proposed new Suffolk County Court House. This, the sixth home for the Law School, became available when the Mt. Vernon Church trustees decided to move to the corner of Massachusetts Avenue and Beacon Street in the new Back Bay. Constructed of Quincy granite—a material so widely used throughout the city in the first quarter of the nineteenth century that the period was called the Granite Age—the old church suited its new academic role perfectly.

On the exterior, it featured an authentic Greek Revival Temple facade of two-story flat pilasters which divided the front into five bays of double windows. Above, a lintel of three narrow courses supported a shallow, full-width triangular pediment. At the apex, between two ACROTERIUM-leaf forms, the university inserted the word "Lex" or law.

The interior reflected the pride of an important Boston congregation. A

double staircase rose to the great 50′ × 75′ second-floor library with its high beamed ceiling. Opposite, a second lecture hall of similar dimensions served as a mock courtroom.

On the third floor, above the library, a magnificent Renaissance Revival–style lecture hall seated 500 persons. Wide paired pilasters with rich CORINTHIAN capitals divided each wall into three compartments and "supported" the great paneled and modillioned COFFER-beams which separated the ceiling into nine sections. In its center, a twenty-foot skylight illuminated the vast space below.

Within these pilasters, a great paneled Roman arch resting on heavy

*11 Ashburton Place. (Boston University Special Collections)*

A corner in the Library.

short piers formed a backdrop for the raised speaker's platform. Thus the decor designed to house the law of the Bible found new dignity as a school for the law of the land.

## A11/688 Boylston Street

Harvard Medical School, Ware and Van Brunt, 1883; 1913, remodeled for Boston University College of Liberal Arts, Arthur Bowditch; 1967, demolished for Boston Public Library addition.

In 1907, Boston University bought the former Harvard Medical School, intending to convert it, as an investment, into offices and shops. On second thought it was decided to use the six-and-a-half-story building to bring together a number of the university's scattered departments under one roof, at a location that had become the very heart of Boston's intellectual life, next door to the new Boston Public Library.

Although the Boston Public Library—designed by McKim, Mead and White and built between 1883 and 1895—was hailed by art critics throughout the world as daringly innovative, its Classical Revival vocabulary, its proportions, and the height of its BELT CORNICES were strikingly similar to those of the adjacent Harvard Medical School, completed in 1883. (One of its designers, Ware, was the first chairman of the Department of Architecture at M.I.T.).

On acquiring the building, Boston University commissioned Arthur

Bowditch (Tours A, B, C, D) to undertake extensive interior renovations and an addition in the Federal Revival style. The feature best remembered by alumni was the popular meeting place, "The Marble," a large foyer paved with slate and marble and dominated by large columns. (A tile of this marble is embedded in the Mugar Memorial Library wall, in the southwest alcove; another is mounted at the entrance.)

In 1935, the Graduate School occupied the Soden Building, a TAPESTRY-BRICK Florentine palazzo, just behind the College of Liberal Arts and along Exeter and Blagdon Streets. After Boston University moved to the Charles River Campus, these properties were acquired by the Boston Public Library; and in the 1970s, they were both torn down to make room for Philip Johnson's new wing of the library.

## A12/264 Huntington Avenue

Repertory Theatre of Boston and Ell Club, J. Williams Beal, 1925; 1953, Boston University Theatre.

The famous Repertory Hall and Club was a landmark in Boston cultural life. The million-dollar building was financed by a group of prominent Bostonians, including Calvin Coolidge and Harvard president A. Lawrence Lowell, to provide a showcase for Henry Jewett, a distinguished Australian actor and the leading man of Julia Marlowe. As the first tax-exempt theatre in the nation, it was thus America's first civic playhouse. According to *The Architect*, "This costly building was a model of modern construction techniques and the most advanced theatre technology"; and with the adjacent Ell Building, it provided space

*(Upper Left) The Law School Library. (From the* Boston University Law School Magazine, *1908)*

*(Lower Left) The Law Lecture Hall. (From the* Boston University Law School Magazine, *1908)*

*688 Boylston Street, showing 1913 addition. (Boston University Special Collections)*

*(Lower Right) "The Marble" at 688 Boylston Street. (Boston University Special Collections)*

for teaching "every phase of stagecraft." The Jewett troupe, however, lasted but five years, a victim to the popularity of motion pictures; and the building itself, rechristened the Esquire Theatre, became an art film house. In 1953, Boston University purchased the theatre and Ell but defrayed the cost by leasing space to the fledgling WGBH-TV. Renovations in 1975 returned the building to its original purpose.

The building is representative of the elegant detail and composition inherent in the Classical Revival vocabulary. Graceful, elliptical-shaped porti-

cos frame the doorways. Their rich detail is handled with great delicacy and restraint. Paired, fluted Corinthian columns with capitals of ACANTHUS leaves and angled VOLUTES support an ENTABLATURE of a running GUILLOCHE pattern and modillion cornice embellished on the underside with MUTULE garnished with knob-like GUTTAE. The center-bay poster-billboards are treated as windows. Fluted pilasters divide the upper facade into three vertical sections; crowned by a PARAPET of open balusters and a closed panel. Recalling the Weld mansion (D15), carved lime-

*264 Huntington Avenue, the Boston University Theatre.*

*Exterior detail of the Boston University Theatre.*

*Interior of the Boston University Theatre.*

stone ornament (here oak leaves) surmount the ceremonial doors and enframe the round window above.

Inside, along with elaborate staircases, Classical ornament in wood, marble, and plaster, in the architect's words, "dignifies and warms" the interior decor. Corinthian pilasters flank the stage and invite the eye upward to the oval cove high in the balcony ceiling where the ubiquitous acorn and oak-leaf motifs abound.

*Tour B—Part One*     **The Cottage Farm
Historic District**

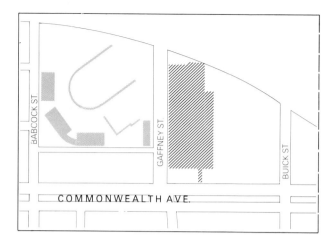

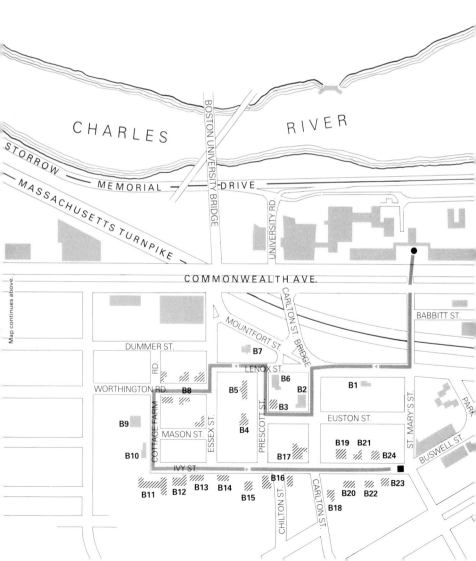

## Tour B—Part One  The Cottage Farm Historic District

● Starting Point of Tour
■ Ending Point of Tour

■▪■ Walking Tour
▨ University Properties

▨ Privately Owned
Properties

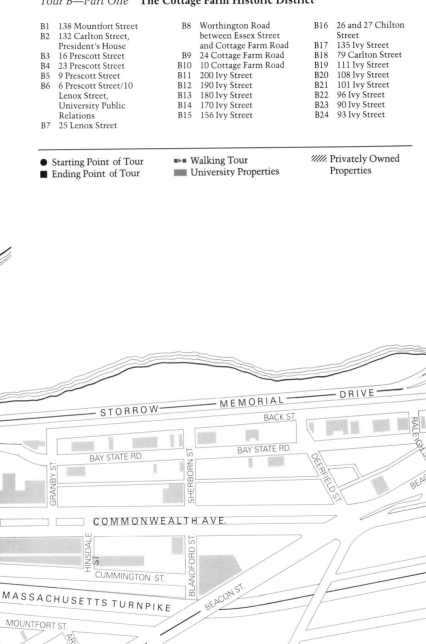

From Marsh Chapel, south over the turnpike and railroad is an area developed from the land holdings of Amos and William Lawrence, pioneers in the textile industry. In 1850, they moved from Boston to Brookline; Amos wrote: ". . . Now we begin to enjoy the country, for [my] house, although it is only two miles from Beacon [Hill] . . . is as much in the country as though it were twenty. . . . [We] have ninety acres and . . . to profit, we hope to see it occupied."

The brothers tightly controlled the development of lots by selling them only to family or friends whom they allowed to build stone or brick summer houses of Gothic or Italianate styles in PICTURESQUE landscaped settings. With the advent of train service from Boston, and the construction of a bridge to Cambridge in the early 1850s, year-round houses began to appear in the later Second Empire style, still classical but with mansard roofs. At the turn of the century, wealthy businessmen updated earlier structures or constructed free-standing houses and mansions in the Queen Anne and Classical Revival styles. The final building phase from about 1911 to World War II saw the introduction of imposing Colonial Revival and English Tudor homes on the remaining land.

The significance of this neighborhood is indicated by its designation as a NATIONAL REGISTER HISTORIC DISTRICT. The size and quality of construction for these buildings are consistent; the dominant materials are stone, brick, and stucco with wood or stone trim. Today, these are the homes of professionals and businesspeople. A few nonprofit institutions have moved into the large mansions but with little exterior alteration. In addition to the six Boston University structures, Tour B presents unusually fine examples of privately owned domestic architecture.

*Map of a section of Cottage Farm, dating from 1888. The future Cottage Farm Road will run through Sears property on left. A gas station now stands on the site of the Cottage Farm Station.*

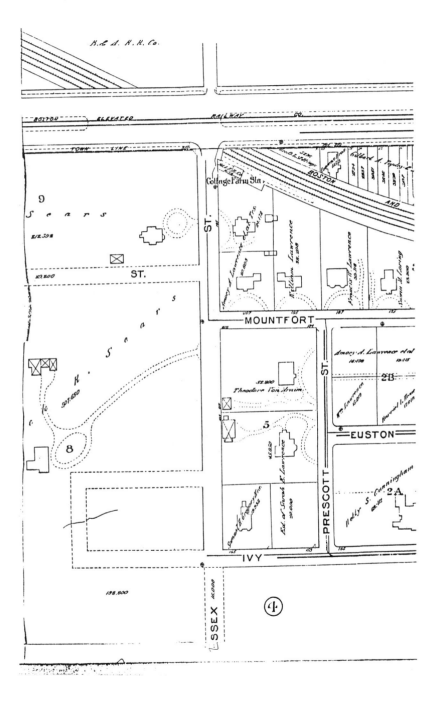

### B1/138 Mountfort Street

Built for Amos A. Lawrence, c. 1855;
occupied by the Boston University
Afro-American Studies Center and
the Graduate Department of
Geography.

The Cottage Style, of which this
building is a fine example, gained
wide acceptance after the 1842 publi-
cation of a book by Andrew Jackson
Downing, *Cottage Residences, Rural
Architecture and Landscape Garden-
ing.* Downing, assisted by Alexander
Jackson Davis and other architects,
popularized the English "NATURAL
LANDSCAPE" and Gothic Revival as a
style for American suburban architecture. David Sears and Amos Lawrence
constructed similar houses on their
"country property."

This small, one-and-a-half-story
cottage provides an excellent example
of the Gothic Revival vocabulary used
to create variety and movement. It has

*138 Mountfort Street.*

a steep, cross-gable roof form. The entrance porch is pierced by a door and
by narrow side windows shaped as
Gothic pointed, lancet arches. Second-
floor wall dormers contain double
windows and, at the third floor, round
ones, which are cruder versions of the
trefoils found at 24 Cottage Farm
Road (B9). A small rear veranda is entered from the dining room through
double doors.

The interior typically blends Gothic
with Italianate Revival forms. Fireplaces feature Gothic elements which
are almost identical to those in the
Angier House built in 1842 in Med-
ford, Massachusetts, by A. J. Davis, a
leading Gothic Revival–style architect. Surrounded by narrow marble
slabs, the fireplaces display a shallow
Tudor arch with scroll motifs at the
shoulders. The original fire basket and
matching grate are still intact in the
east bedroom. Italianate features include door moldings and chandelier
ceiling rosettes.

*132 Carlton Street.*

## B2/132 Carlton Street

Kilham and Hopkins, 1908; home of the President of Boston University.

Designed to face two streets, this cream-colored stucco, three-story mansion sits with solid dignity on a corner site. Five bays by five bays, it illustrates the classical French-inspired symmetrical pavilion form. The influence of the French ECOLE DES BEAUX ARTS was locally adopted in the much heralded Boston Public Library (1888) by McKim, Mead and White; and the style achieved national exposure and instant popularity at the 1893 World Columbian Exposition in Chicago.

Decoration emphasizes the center doorway and building outlines. Vertical stone quoins boldly delineate the corners contrasting with the strong horizontal modillion cornice. On the slate roof with its segmental dormers, chimneys punctuate the end bays at the junctions with the central section, further defining the pavillion form. The massing of this house is almost identical to the neighboring #122 which was designed in the Federal Revival mode. The doorway here at #132 is approached by a short flight of stairs. Heavy, rusticated half-round ENGAGED columns with a large bracketed entablature above frame this doorway. Paired end bays and a second-story porch in the rear wing characterize the south Euston Street facade. The service-entrance facade on the north side is functional and thus asymmetrical.

### B3/16 Prescott Street

Corner Euston Street, Joseph C. Chandler, 1906. Private.

Typical of the Tudor Revival style is the massing of this red-brick mansion. Note also the open Jacobean style STRAPWORK with balustrade over the entrance, the stone-trimmed gables, and the brick wall and gateway with Egyptian PYLON ornament.

This choice of Tudor illustrates the broad taste for historic styles among clients. Chandler was also an authority on Colonial architecture and was involved in the restoration of three major American "icons": the Paul Revere House, the House of Seven Gables, and the Old Corner Bookstore.

*Gateway, 16 Prescott Street.*

### B4/23 Prescott Street

Wells-Catlin House, 1868–71. Private.

Still in its original condition, this outstanding example of high-style Second Empire serves as an illustrative foil to its remodeled neighbors (B5, B7, B20, B22, B23). The curves of the pent roof, dormers, window hoods, and deep corbeled cornice animate the imposing square facade. The strong, projecting polygonal entrance bay serves as a transition between the faster rhythm of the cornice and the more stately large window openings of the side bays. Classical details of brick abound in the belt cornice dividing the lower floors, and in the brackets and corner quoins.

### B5/9 Prescott Street

Corner Euston Street; Lawrence house, 1855; 1902, remodeled for E. P. Fish, Winslow and Bigelow; 1973, rear addition for New England Hebrew Academy, Amy Du Pont. Private.

As originally constructed, this house was dominated by a high mansard roof characteristic of Cottage Farm residences built from the late 1850s through the 1870s. In the turn-of-the-century remodeling for the president of American Telephone and Telegraph Company, the architects created an impressive mansion in the Colonial Revival style. They raised the mansard attic level to a full third story, replaced window sash, and added side wings. At the rear, they erected a GIANT-ORDER, paired-column portico which, fortunately, is not obscured by the academy classroom addition.

## B6/6 Prescott Street

10 Lenox Street, Curtis Mansion, Prescott and Sidebottom, 1904; Boston University Public Relations.

The animated exterior exhibits many elements of the late-nineteenth-century Queen Anne Revival style made fashionable by the well-publicized English country houses of Richard Norman Shaw, with a medieval vocabulary of vast, complicated roof forms, mock HALF-TIMBER and stucco upper stories, a wide OVERHANG, and clustered chimney shapes. Windows come in a bewildering variety, from single to quadruple sets, some with small panes above, others with stained glass within a transom arrangement. On the rear elevation, a broad PORTE-COCHERE reaches out from the entrance porch while, beside it, a huge two-story window announces the great stair hall within.

Inside, the rambling floor plan indicates the influence of the English Domestic Revival and focuses on the great two-story LIVING HALL, here dominated by American Colonial Re-

*6 Prescott Street.*

vival motifs. The ceremonial divided staircase with its encircling balcony repeats the variety of carved SPINDLES. This elaborate historical detail refers to Boston's eighteenth-century John Hancock House, torn down amid great public outcry in 1863. Dividing the foyer from the great living hall is a Palladian triple opening, an arch with columns set within a broader shallow arch, again a motif frequently employed along Bay State Road (Tour D).

The principal front rooms continue the English Tudor feeling of the exterior. At the far end of the dark paneled and beamed dining room, a raised IN-GLENOOK alcove nestles alongside the fireplace. The chimneypiece of the paneled and beamed living room displays diamond-shaped panels with octagonal pillars around which ropes of laurel leaves entwine, while the "morning room" combines Tudor-style transom windows and stained-glass insets with high, paneled moldings and brackets.

49

*23 Prescott Street.*

*9 Prescott Street.*

*25 Lenox Street.*

*108 Ivy Street.*

Delicate ADAMESQUE plaster designs in the great coffered living-hall ceiling find full expression in the former music room where curving wall moldings and the richly swagged mirror of the fireplace and OVERMANTLE create a sophisticated elegance. Such "feminine" rooms were common in these turn-of-the-century mansions (Tour D, especially D8, 18b, 29) and reflected the new taste for the delicacy and restraint of the Classical French Beaux Arts style expounded by the tastemakers Edith Wharton and Ogden Codman.

### B7/25 Lenox Street

Built for Amos A. Lawrence, c. 1855; 1874/1900/1925, renovations; University housing.

The seventeenth-century French Baroque style adopted by Emperor Napoleon III for his new mid-nineteenth-century Paris, in particular, the Louvre, inspired many of Amos Lawrence's houses. The Deacon House (1848–71) in Boston's New South End, by the French architect Jean Lemoulnier had already introduced the mansard roof with its flat top and steep sides. Six houses on this tour all feature a projecting center entry porch flanked by double windows, brick construction, and mansard roofs. Later renovations here and at B5 and B23 added a third full story.

For over 130 years, the exterior of the three bay, two-and-a-half-story brick center section of this house has remained unaltered. Built by Amos Lawrence, it is similar to those he commissioned in the Second Empire style at 90, 96, and 108 Ivy Street (B23, 22, 20) as well as 23 and 9 Prescott Street (B4, 5) across the street. Over-

sized paired windows balance symmetrically on the facade. The projecting entrance porch, set within a segmental arch with KEYSTONE, adds interest to the front, whose strong verticals expressed in the tall windows are resolved by a heavy cornice crowned by a mansard roof. There is restrained decoration in the form of stone lintels and sills, the gray slate mansard roof and modillion cornice.

Owners added a porch in 1874 and an east bay in 1900. In 1925, they embarked upon a major interior renovation, adopting the Colonial Revival style of the newer construction in the neighborhood (B8, 11, 12). Nationally, at this time, there was a strong interest in accurate reproduction of past architectural forms, which culminated in the founding of Colonial Williamsburg.

### B8/Worthington Road between Essex Street and Cottage Farm Road

Private.

This streetscape illustrates the later styles popular in the periods when construction filled the last empty lots. In 1911–13, both the English Tudor and Georgian Revival styles found favor and continued to be utilized up to World War II.

**3, 4 Worthington Road**   Berry and Davidson, 1916.

Extreme simplification in the Federal Revival style with emphasis upon repetition; flat brick surfaces with wooden trim and prominent center bays create a sense of great solidity.

**11 Worthington Road**   Harry Ramsay (B16), 1942.

A simpler, one-story version but with the metal casement windows popular in that period.

**12 Worthington Road**   Frank Bourne, 1911.

English Domestic Revival style with segmental-arched brick windows, white wooden trim, and prominent wall gables.

**43 Cottage Farm Road**   J. L. Little, 1912.

Note the English cottage effect achieved by the use of stucco and a curved, pent-roof shape.

**22 Worthington Road**   Andrews, Jacques and Rantoul, 1913

This prominent Boston firm highlighted the rich limestone-carved door enframement with spare, restrained window trim against a red-brick wall surface. Robert Day Andrews, the senior partner, trained at M.I.T. and, later, under the great architect Henry Hobson Richardson. The Andrews firm, best known for the wing-additions to the Massachusetts State House, designed offices, banks, and private residences.

## B9/24 Cottage Farm Road

George M. Dexter (?), architect, for Frederick Sears, 1848–52; 1910, interior remodeled for Fritz Talbot; 1960, University housing.

This imposing Italianate/Gothic Revival house is among the most historic buildings in Brookline. It stands on a curving drive amid spacious grounds which, in their day, imitated the picturesque "natural" English country-park style promoted by Andrew Jackson Downing. While the bulk of the stone house is Italianate, the Gothic Revival vocabulary is apparent in the porches and the top story. Perhaps Frederick Sears, the first developer of the Cottage Farm area, encountered Downing's book of 1842 and changed his mind part way through construction. The details in this house are expensive and contrast with the more modest period examples encountered along the tour.

Italianate structural details in the first two stories include symmetrical spacing of single, oversized windows with curving consoles supporting a hood MOLDING, the stone balustrades under the upstairs windows, and heavy quoin blocks outlining the corners of the house. Gothic Revival elements, however, dominate the facade's projecting decoration and uppermost story. There is typical irregular massing of building form and roof shapes (cf. B1). All four sides feature steep gables with trefoil or quatrefoil windows. Open, sawn VERGEBOARD trims the eaves. The right front jerkinhead gable breaks the symmetry of the lower floors. The Gothic impression is completed with the clustered chimneys with their round pots and the shallow Tudor arches of the stone porches.

The interior is lavishly ornamented, not in the Gothic but the Italianate mode. Heavy, paired columns and pilasters divide the outer and inner halls and support a rich, classical entablature of TRIGLYPH and METOPE. The high ceilings carry a series of wide moldings and an elaborate plaster chandelier MEDALLION. The dining room fireplace mantel is supported by a broad, curving black-marble CONSOLE. The cast-iron grate blends styles: it features hexagonal posts embellished with Gothic details, the only Gothic ornament inside the house.

In 1910, the new owner, Dr. Fritz Talbot (no relation to Dr. Israel Talbot, A4) redecorated the front entry, parlor, and music room in a more chaste Colonial Revival style. The Talbots sold their home to the university in 1960. Some of the furnishings which give character to the interior were acquired from the Talbots.

## B10/10 Cottage Farm Road

Markus and Nocka, 1939; home of University chaplain.

The archaeological correctness of 1930s reproductions extended even to more modest suburban Federal Revival houses. This example was built next door to the home of Dr. Fritz Talbot by his son, Dr. Nathan Talbot, an internationally known pediatrician.

A two-story center-entrance home, it employs Colonial details in the pilaster-pediment door enframement, in the narrow side windows which recall the Palladian triple window form, and in the shutters. The service wing and garage are modern adaptations for

*24 Cottage Farm Road.*

twentieth-century needs, as is the construction of only one chimney, now a decorative rather than heating device.

The privately-owned mansions around Mason Park represent the fourth period of building in the area, the late Colonial Revival. They are, for the most part, massive in scale. Numbers 200 and 190 are quite similar although built in different materials and ten years apart. These two now serve as quarters for the Massachusetts Association for the Blind.

**B11**  200 Ivy Street, John Ames, Georgian Revival, stucco, 1911.

**B12**  190 Ivy Street, William Mowll, Georgian Revival, brick pavilion shape, 1918.

**B13**  180 Ivy Street, Bogner and Billings, 1928.

Georgian Revival door treatment combines Federal Revival style with recessed BLIND ARCHES in the flanking wings. This is a small one-and-a-half-story brick building, but its quality of ornamentation assures its compatibility with its larger neighbors.

*Gable, 24 Cottage Farm Road.*

## B14/170 Ivy Street

Arthur Bowditch, 1912. Private.

Skillful use of English motifs creates a domestic feeling. Bowditch combines a brick Tudor doorway with an overhanging "thatched roof" cottage shape and double medieval gables. He pays homage to the early work of Richard Norman Shaw, one of the founders of the Queen Anne style. Shaw's later Georgian Revival and neo-Baroque influence is seen along Bay State Road.

## B15/156 Ivy Street

George M. Dexter, architect, for Amos A. Lawrence, 1851. Private.

The model of an English manor house in a spacious park setting enhances the significance of the Cottage Farm Historic District as an early suburban experiment. While its form is similar to the more modest builder's cottages at 138 Mountfort (B1) and 89 Carlton (B18), its scale and use of stone create a more massive, monumental effect. Dexter, a well known mid-century Boston architect, was the Lawrences' favorite designer. The three-bay form highlights an enclosed central stone

*170 Ivy Street.*

porch whose stained-glass window is surmounted by a shield bearing "1851." At the top level, small wall dormers flank a central jerkinhead dormer. The powerful GAMBREL-shaped end facades feature a single large square window on each floor. Here, Dexter chose dressed stone to ornament the window frames and prominent corner quoin blocks.

### B16/26 and 27 Chilton Street

Harry Ramsay, 1933 and 1935. Private.

This pair of typical English Tudor Revival houses features stone trim,

asymmetrical massing, and clustered chimneys. Compare with 16 Prescott (B3).

### B17/135 Ivy Street

George M. Dexter, architect, for Amos A. Lawrence, 1851. Private.

Grander even than #156 (B15) across the street, this stone house masses wings, gables, chimneys, and porches into a medieval fantasy. The eastern wing, built a decade and a half later, commemorates the defeat of the Confederacy, with the following inscrip-

*156 Ivy Street.*

*Inscription, 135 Ivy Street.*

tion carved into the stone chimney foundation:

RICH. VICT. APR. III.
A.D. MDCCCLXV.

This prominent chimney divides the narrow, rectangular first-floor windows and round openings in the gable into a neat, integrated composition.

### B18/79 Carlton Street

For Amos A. Lawrence, c. 1855. Private.

The similarity between this stone-and-brick Gothic Revival cottage and that at 138 Mountfort Street (B1) is very strong.

### B19/111 Ivy Street

1855; 1899, remodeled, O'Neal Builders. Private.

On the northeast corner of Ivy, note the large Tudor-style house, atypical

of the work of Howe and Manning. Among the first women graduates of M.I.T. School of Architecture, they specialized in suburban and country homes and were particularly noted for their remodeling of older houses into the then fashionable Colonial Revival mode.

In remodelling 111 Ivy, the O'Neals retained the segmental arched windows and the projecting ORIEL WINDOW framed by a heavy cornice and bottom panels. The new doorway combines narrow, attenuated, fluted IONIC pilasters, a heavy triangular pediment, and a unique leaded-glass TRACERY pattern in the transom and side lights.

A heavy wooden entablature with dentil moldings forms a base of the new Colonial-style attic dormers. O'Neal further altered the original symmetry of the west elevation by introducing a center-bay RECESSED ARCH between the first and second levels. A Regency-style iron balcony (cf. D23) frames this arch and probably opened into the stair landing.

The success of this rebuilding, which almost completely disguises the origins, lies in the basic classical inspiration of both the original structure and its later Colonial Revival embellishment.

### B20/108 Ivy Street

1855, residence for Amos A. Lawrence, c. 1870. Private.

Compare this three-bay, three-story brick, mansard-roof house with double Italianate-style windows on the first floor with B6. Note also its similarity to B4, 22, and 23. Here at #108, a later Colonial Revival–style remodeling altered the first and third floors.

### B21/101 Ivy Street

Residence, Andrews, Jacques and Rantoul, 1892. Private.

Toward the end of the century, a restrained Queen Anne Revival–style brick-and-shingle house took its place among the earlier classical, balanced structures. Asymmetrical, #101 incorporates a variety of roofs, windows, and room sizes. The sawtooth trim on the bottom edge of the overhang is a typical motif used by Boston architects, in particular, H. H. Richardson.

His influence permeated design through the preceding decades; Andrews had trained in his office.

### B22, B23/96 and 90 Ivy Street

Residences for Amos A. Lawrence, c. 1855. Private.

These two brick mansard-roof houses should also be compared with B5, 7, and 20; behind their various alterations is the same basic mansard structure.

### B24/93 Ivy Street

Residence; 1903, remodeled; 1907/22, remodeled by William C. Chase. Private.

The most recent remodeling of this turn-of-the-century house adopted the

*111 Ivy Street.*

popular Federal Revival style of contemporary houses in the neighbor-

hood. Note the stucco finish and the side entrance.

*101 Ivy Street.*

*Tour B—Part Two*    **The South Campus**

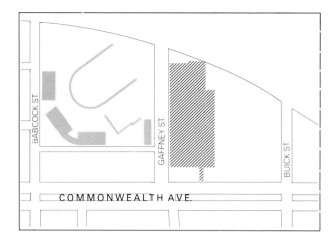

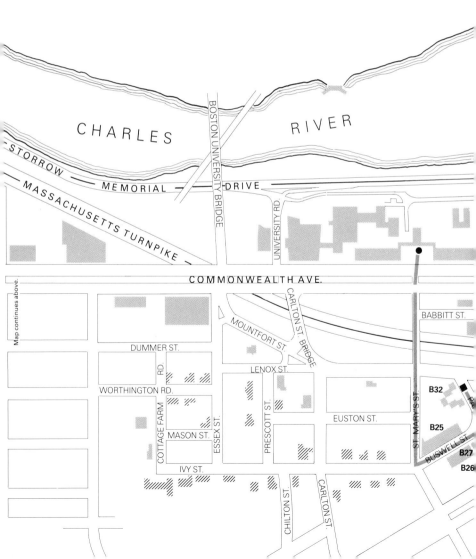

Map continues above.

B25 29–55 Buswell Street   B28 509 Park Drive        B31 3 Buswell Street
B26 38 Buswell Street       B29 22–24 Buswell Street  B32 514–522 Park Drive
B27 500 Park Drive          B30 14 Buswell Street

● Starting Point of Tour   ▪▶▪ Walking Tour           ▨ Privately Owned
■ Ending Point of Tour     ▨ University Properties        Properties

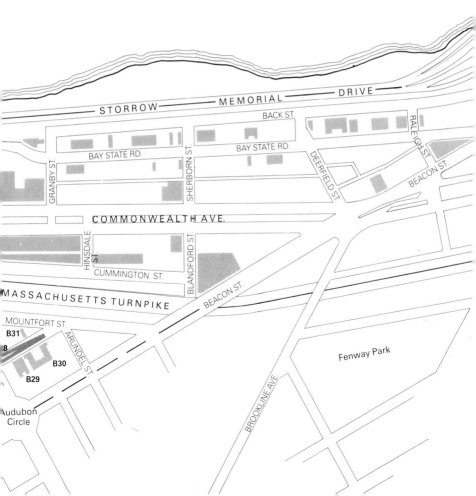

Continuing east on Ivy Street, the tour route crosses the Boston City Line where Ivy is renamed Buswell Street. Here Buswell and Park (formerly Audubon) Drive represent the small-scale, middle-class residential development planned by the Lawrence family for the urban portion of their properties. In the 1870s, soon after landscape architect Frederick Law Olmsted drained the marshes which separated this peninsula from Boston, the land east of St. Mary's Street was transferred from Brookline to the City of Boston. In 1887, the West End Streetcar Company extended service along the newly widened Beacon Street. With householders now pouring out of Boston, the Lawrences subdivided their holdings into narrow house lots. Evidently, they did not object to urban density alongside their nearby suburban estates.

Typical of the builder/speculator of the period was George Wheatland, who quickly purchased lots on Buswell and the entire north sides of Mountfort and Beacon Streets. Wheatland, who also built rowhouses along Bay State Road, worked in a cutthroat market. Builders had to judge carefully the amount of ornamentation that would attract buyers, yet allow them to clear a profit. Detail concentrated around doors, windows, and fireplaces. Staircases displayed finely turned machine-made spindles and wooden paneling. Builders borrowed heavily from established styles, often combining several into one building, thus safely appealing to a broad middle-class market.

To ensure that the prominent corner locations facing Park Drive would be designed in an impressive manner, the Lawrences did not sell them until the end of the century. By the early 1900s the new large brownstone and brick apartment buildings facing Park Drive featured careful massing around the curving corners. These added dignity to the area and framed the smaller, solidly built Classical Revival rowhouses.

As these properties were originally speculative, they continued to change hands over the years. The rowhouses were subdivided into apartments and then rooming houses. In 1979, Boston University began converting these buildings into student housing. University landscaping, maintenance, and security have brought stability into the neighborhood.

## B25/29–55 Buswell Street

Rowhouses, Samuel D. Kelley for Warren Vinal, 1896; University dormitories. 31 and 33 privately owned.

Warren Vinal, brother of city architect Arthur Vinal (B31, C5, D6, 7), was also involved on nearby Bay State Road as a rowhouse builder-speculator. Though the Buswell and Beacon Street homes were designed for a less-affluent market, the builders still strove to maintain a modicum of style within their tight budget.

This block of three-and-a-half-story bowfront rowhouses of tan brick and brownstone trim reflects Colonial Revival design and materials. Ornamentation focuses around the door and above the windows on the first two levels. Colonial molding designs frame the doorway and glass transom. Vinal uses a simple door of natural

wood with a single panel below and beveled glass above.

Inside, the builder adapts the formality of larger townhouses to a smaller scale in the mosaic floor and paneled WAINSCOTING of the vestibule. He retains their grander floor plans with the large wainscoted interior hall, which receives air and light through double doors, opening ENFILADE to the front and back rooms. Other than a fireplace, however, there is limited ornament.

Decoration is used where it will have the greatest impact in the central living hall. Here, the three-stage split staircase, top lit by a red-and-blue glass skylight, is the imposing element. The machine-carved NEWEL POST and RAMP RAIL overshadow the plain stock spindles, three to a tread.

Details are even more lavish on the

*29–55 Buswell Street.*

hall fireplace. Typical of the Colonial Revival style are the small ceramic tiles enframing the opening and pillars with Corinthian capitals supporting the mantle shelf, above which is an oval mirrored overmantle with decorative molding and side scrolls. This standard decorative formula can be found in other speculator rowhouses here on the South Campus and along upper Bay State Road.

### B26/38 Buswell Street

Apartments, D. H. Woodbury, 1911; University dormitories.

This Federal Revival apartment house adds to the mix of residential building styles popular in the South Campus area. Although Woodbury paid careful attention to exterior detail, the building barely echoes the expensive townhouses on nearby Bay State Road. The brick is laid in FLEMISH BOND with dark HEADERS alternating with red STRETCHERS; white limestone quoins frame the doorway. Other ornament includes stone pediments, belt courses, and detail above the windows. Recently, the university modernized the doorway and removed the number "38" incorporated in the stained-glass door transom, which had added a touch of luxury to the otherwise restrained building.

The entry continues the custom of a mosaic tile floor. Behind the elaborate door, however, the plain tiled hall and simple staircase indicate the modesty of the developer's budget.

### B27/500 Park Drive

Apartments, Benjamin Fox, 1903; University dormitory.

"Audubon Terrace" was praised in its day for cleverly overcoming the difficulties of a lot of singular shape. In fact, the excitement of the double building is found in the way in which

*500 Park Drive.*

the architect massed round and square shapes and grouped windows to curve around the corner while still giving the appearance from two sides of a solid block.

Almost a mirror image of its twin at 503 Park Drive, the red-brick-and-brownstone exterior reflects the late-nineteenth-century Romanesque style designs of H. H. Richardson. Heavy rusticated brownstone blocks dramatize the basement and the carefully proportioned first floor. Brownstone further outlines the wide arched doorway with windows above, the oval window on each side, the double transomed windows, and the projecting side BAY WINDOW. Carving on the doorway and the base of the projecting bay is a typical curving-leaf motif.

On the second and third floors, window openings become smaller, and the spacing and doubling echo the dramatic window treatment on the main level. The modillion cornice and decorative interior woodwork is in the Co-

lonial Revival style—testifying to the eclectic nature of the design. Such detailing, however, was limited by a budget of $18,500 for a building 40 feet long, 35 feet wide, and 37 feet high.

### B28/509 Park Drive

Apartments, Norcross Brothers, 1912; University dormitory.

The "Plymouth" apartments illustrate the sort of design executed by a prominent construction firm which provides its own architectural service. Since no architect is listed on the building permit, Norcross Bros. probably provided appropriate expertise. According to James O'Gorman (quoted in Wodehouse), they were "without question among the most important construction companies in the U. S. in the late 19th and early 20th centuries. They executed at least half the designs of H. H. Richardson."

*509 Park Drive.*

*22–24 Buswell Street.*

The firm produced woodwork, stone-work, and interior fittings as well as exterior construction. Here, many decades after Richardson, Norcross worked in a Colonial Revival mode and on a limited budget.

The shape is well suited to its curving site. The building rests upon what appears to be a solid base: the effect of heavy stone blocks is imitated economically by projecting every seventh row of bricks. The vertical emphasis upon the ornamental central entrance bay and flanking polygonal bays breaks up the great mass of the structure. A heavy, segmental stone arch, supported by carved consoles and garnished with floral swags, frames the doorway. Above, a pair of windows faced with limestone rests within an arched hood, supported by yet another set of curving bracket/consoles. The present front door, unfortunately, is a poor replacement.

Inside, natural oak woodwork embellishes the Colonial Revival hallway and stairwell. Dentil trim above the doors, paneled dado, and Georgian-style stair balusters give a rich effect. The architects failed, however, to solve the organization of interior space in a curving building and squan-dered it on oversized, though decorated, public halls.

### B29/22–24 Buswell Street

Tenement for C. R. Beals, 1914; University dormitory.

The 1914 building permit called for construction of 24 "family tenements." The result is an economical, double building of two three-by-three bay sections with center entrances. All windows are double, creating a sense of light and space in the small interior rooms. Although there is a hint of Tudor in the castle-like crenellation over the third-floor windows, the doorways and windows are Colonial Revival. In addition, the roof parapet and diamond shapes below are similar to the "modern" commercial garage facades built at the same time on Cummington Street. The speculator-builder appealed to all tastes!

### B30/14 Buswell Street

Apartments, S. W. Jacobs, 1924; University dormitory.

This five-and-a-half-story, U-shaped, luxury apartment building is a form of housing which became increasingly popular in the mid-1920s. Built for $250,000, it is in sharp contrast to the corner apartments at 509 Park Drive, which were constructed twelve years earlier at a cost of only $80,000. Here, the stylistic features imitate those of the luxury Federal Revival townhouses along Bay State Road.

The street-ends of the wings receive special attention as pavilion forms. Here, double windows feature flat stone balconies while a pediment shape capped in stone crowns the roofline above. Classical vocabulary in contrasting limestone defines the tan brick shape. The ground floor is rusticated; quoins outline the corners. Corner panels feature an Adamesque design and center panel.

A major feature of the front elevation is the stone enframement of the main entrance. Two-story classical pilasters supporting a heavy lintel flank the wide door; deep-cut egg-and-dart

molding surrounds the frame. Above the lintel is a simple dentil entablature upon which rest the third-floor windows. The surrounding wall is faced in limestone and garnished with free-standing urns. The flanking wings achieve clarity through the spare rhythm of the patterns of rectangular windows. The effect is one of innate modesty, severity, and restraint.

## B31/3 Buswell Street

Rowhouse, Arthur Vinal, 1894; University dormitory.

A sure command of the Colonial Revival idiom is evident in this pair of red brick and limestone bowfront townhouses. The architect, Arthur Vinal, who was city architect a decade earlier, designed the "most correct townhouses" for speculation along Bay State Road (Tour D). Speculation involved erecting a building with

*14 Buswell Street.*

*3 Buswell Street.*

one's own money, investing only enough in ornament to attract the buyer.

Vinal focused his efforts on the entrance, with its rich but restrained ornamentation. The paneled door is set within narrow wooden pilasters which support a delicately leaded segmental-arched transom. The swelling BOW WINDOWS balance the heavy front steps.

The Colonial Revival interior treatment echoes that found in speculator townhouses along Bay State Road. Al-

though the staircase reflects Vinal's interest in authentic eighteenth-century models, the various spindle patterns are common STOCK moldings. The popular Queen Anne Revival "Sunburst" motif shines forth, carved into the newel post above the rail joint.

### B32/514–522 Park Drive

Apartment buildings, Arthur Bowditch, 1915; University dormitories.

*514–522 Park Drive.*

Similar to the large free-standing houses on the Cottage Farm portion of this tour, this apartment complex employs the Tudor Revival style (B3, 8, 16). For this commission, the symmetrical plan of the architect Arthur Bowditch expresses its residential purpose in the U-shaped arrangement of the three units, which allows large windows on all the facades. By clustering the buildings, he adapts to the corner site while retaining a central courtyard.

The building's design utilizes Tudor detail without being coldly academic. Exterior ornament concentrates on the center doorways and on the windows and rooflines. The elaborate three-story central bay imitates a castle gatehouse and displays a stone pediment with two heraldic coats-of-arms. On the second floor, a broad, pointed-arch window repeats the stone tab hood molding over the doorway. On the third floor, a square arch with FINIAL surmounts a square-headed window with blank pointed-arch. Along the eaves-line, an elabo-

rate balustrade incorporates mythical beasts bearing shields. A molded cornice and heavy lintel terminate the active composition and continue along the flanking wings. White, stone-framed windows reiterate the Tudor motif.

In the interior, the owners abandoned the formidable Tudor Revival motifs for a more comfortable Colonial Revival design. The four-room suites have minimal ornament: outline moldings to form panels on the living room walls and a built-in china cupboard with finely detailed glass doors in the compact dining room.

*Tour C*

# The Charles River Campus

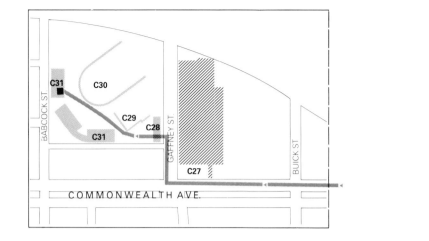

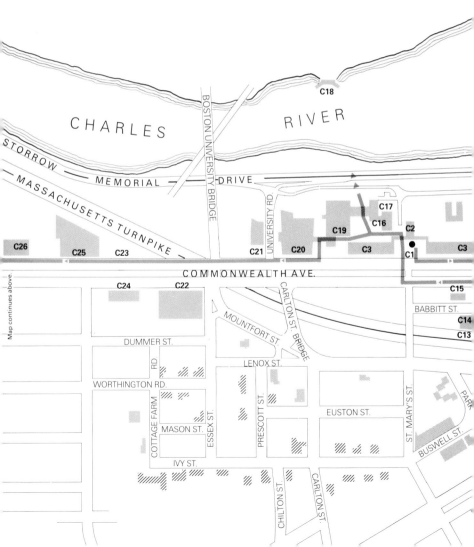

## Tour C  The Charles River Campus

● Starting Point of Tour
■ Ending Point of Tour

▪▶▪ Walking Tour
▨ University Properties

▨▨ Privately Owned Properties

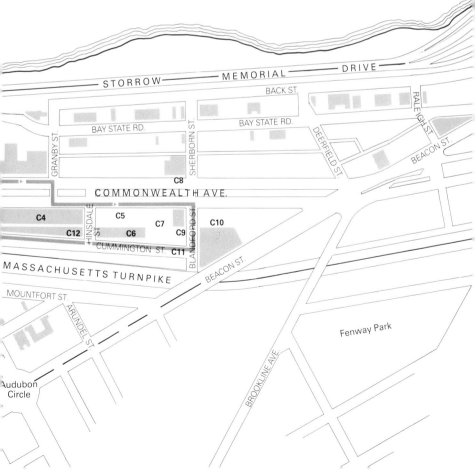

The Main Campus along Commonwealth Avenue was built on the last available open tract of land in west Boston—130,000 square feet of upland and an acre of underwater tidal flats. By 1909, the Riverbank Improvement Association, headed by Charles Frances Adams and his son, John Quincy Adams, Jr., descendants of presidents of the United States, had purchased the whole of this tract from Ebeneezer Francis (the owner of the Buswell Street property, Tour B). As befitted its name, the association's first step was to improve the riverbank by filling in the flats out to a line drawn along the bank by the Harbor Commissioners in 1876. (The granite-block retaining wall the association erected along this line is still in use along the south side of Storrow Drive.) Fill for the project came from the excavations for the Kenmore (then Governor's) Square subway station.

The association controlled property designs through deed restrictions on setbacks and projections, materials and building types. Apartment buildings could not be built for ten years beginning in 1889, nor could stables be erected; and because of the 80-foot height limitation, Boston University was able, at a later date, to obtain this land for half its market value. (After its bargain purchase, the university secured a height variance of up to 155 feet.)

The new Charles River Campus was a project dear to the heart of President Daniel Marsh, who spent much time and energy in a loving elaboration of its details. Cram and Ferguson, one of the country's most illustrious architectural firms, had drawn up a master plan for the campus.

*The wavy line at top of chart indicates the low-water mark, which was to be filled to form part of the Charles River Campus. The dotted Harbor Line was to become the route of the present Storrow Drive. (From an 1890 chart courtesy Suffolk County Court House)*

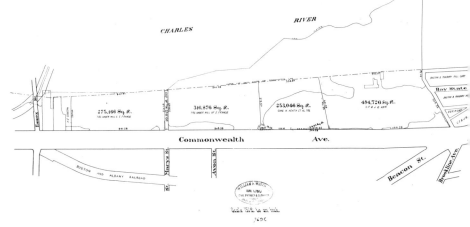

*The Cram-Coolidge proposal—the Commonwealth Avenue façade. (Courtesy Hoyle, Doran and Berry)*

The architects were noted for their success in adapting neo-Gothic designs to modern tastes and requirements (among their buildings were those at the United States Military Academy at West Point). For Boston University, they created a series of plans based on a set of interconnecting quadrangles, after the fashion of the Oxford colleges. One early plan, conceived in the RENAISSANCE style, consisted of seven-story buildings with shallow tiled roofs, arranged in quadrangles and encircling a central, domed structure, similar to Cram's Baltimore Cathedral. (The choice of red brick for the buildings revealed the architect's sensitivity to the brick townhouses on adjacent Bay State Road.)

In another neo-Gothic version, Cram turned to the concept of a central administrative tower, flanked by buildings forming cathedral-like naves. (This concept was particularly appealing to President Murlin and the trustees, who had nurtured the idea of a landmark tower to be named in honor of the late Professor Alexander Graham Bell.) In this plan, massive square towers and great entrance portals emphasized the corners and end facades.

These master plans suffered a fatal blow in 1929, when the Metropolitan District Commission took 130,000 square feet of the university's riverside frontage by eminent domain for the Storrow Embankment Park, thereby separating the campus from the river. This separation was dramatically emphasized in 1951 by the construction of Storrow Drive.

*The Charles River Campus in 1942, viewed from the roof of 808 Commonwealth Avenue. (Boston University Special Collections)*

Of Cram's original designs, only those for the Commonwealth Avenue side of the proposed quadrangles ever came to be built.

Over the years, other designs were considered to fill in the uncompleted portion of the Cram master plan. Each reflected changing architectural fashion rather than a sympathetic response to the original plan, and it is perhaps fortunate that none were grafted onto the existing scheme. It remained for José Luis Sert, in the late 1950s, to reorient the buildings dramatically toward the river and to provide a new heart for the campus.

All the while, the campus continued to grow outside the original tract. Located in the midst of automobile salesrooms and factories served by Commonwealth Avenue and the nearby railroad tracks, the university had access to a substantial amount of potential floor space which it could acquire as its needs arose. Although such renovations were costly, no demolition was required. Such ADAPTIVE REUSE halted the blight which occurred as, one by one, tenants abandoned these buildings. Usually, the university redesigned both the facades and the interiors. Where auto showrooms had extensive ornate detail, these details were carefully retained.

**C1/Marsh Plaza** (in front of 735 Commonwealth Avenue), **Martin Luther King, Jr., Memorial**

Sergio Castillo, sculptor

The memorial to Dr. Martin Luther King, Jr., distinguished graduate of Boston University, consists of a series of birdlike shapes formed from curved metal plates. These "birds" flock together in an upward direction. Together, they create a larger, soaring

*Marsh Chapel and the Martin Luther King, Jr., Memorial.*

form which reaches upward as a symbol of hope. Quotations from Dr. King occupy three sides of the stone base.

**C2/735 Commonwealth Avenue, The Marsh Chapel**

1939–48, Cram and Ferguson/Coolidge, Shepley, Bullfinch and Abbott.

Set back at the head of Ashby Street, the nineteenth-century approach to the Charles River bridge, the Marsh Chapel forms the center of the campus, both physically and spiritually.

Its architect, Ralph Adams Cram, wrote in reference to the chapel he designed at Princeton University:

> The chapel should epitomize, glorify the whole architectural quality of the university. It must be in spirit and in form all that is possible at the hands of the architects and university . . . a great and lasting example of religious art, linked with the highest standards of secular education. . . . It must strike some workable balance between archeology and creative art. Every effort has been made to obtain an effect of dignity and impressiveness through the grandeur of mass and the simplicity of form.

The Marsh Chapel was constructed of Indiana limestone at a cost of almost one million dollars. Massive bronze double doors, recessed within a series of pointed arches, dominate the facade. Above, a great window repeats the entrance shapes and announces the religious function of the building. Strong buttresses frame the corners while the sides alternate these same pointed arch windows and buttresses.

The interior space consists of a single, lofty NAVE with no transepts, offering the congregation unobstructed vision and hearing. Spare decoration of deeply carved QUARTER-GRAIN English oak is carefully positioned for the greatest effect. Stained glass by the gifted artist Charles Connick depicts doorways representing four major religions: the Methodist church of the founders by the City Church in London, the Protestants by the Cathedral at Wittenberg, the Roman Catholic by St. Peter's in Rome, and the Jewish by Solomon's Temple in Jerusalem. Throughout, Cram incorporated window tracery from the former School of Theology on Chestnut Street (A8). The screen behind the altar contains figures surrounded by lavish pinnacles. Carved Gothic wooden TRUSSES embellish the ceiling, where chande-

liers display the Boston University seal in red and white. The overall effect is restrained treatment of the neo-Gothic vocabulary.

The chapel is sited between two classroom blocks and is connected to them by covered ARCADES. The architect thus provides a CLOISTER and further reinforces the sense of a medieval scholastic community.

Echoing the chapel are two small but different neo-Gothic towers. Only a trace of the Gothic remains in these abstracted modern forms, which are too small in scale for the mass of the building. The landmark tower can still be seen, however, as sculpture set in the overdoor transoms of the entrances to the classroom blocks.

## C3/755–675 Commonwealth Avenue

1939–48, Cram and Ferguson/Coolidge, Shepley, Bulfinch and Abbott, University classroom and administration buildings.

The rapid construction of Charles Hayden Memorial, the first component of the Charles River Campus (now 685 Commonwealth Avenue), imposed a design choice upon the master plan. Cram and Ferguson, proponents of the Gothic Style, collaborated with Coolidge, Shepley, Bulfinch and Abbott, the successor firm to H. H. Richardson. Both were leaders in campus design. From 1933 to 1935, the Coolidge group had also worked on a major project, the New York Hospital of Cornell Medical College.

Boston University's sheer facade, the use of metal spandrels between metal-sash windows to create vertical fenestration terminating in pointed arches, and the taller nave-like windows at the top story are all strikingly similar to New York Hospital. In fact, in 1938, the same firm designed a new building with similar, but abstracted, vertical fenestration at Northeastern University, a few blocks west of the Copley Square Campus.

Over a ten-year period, a giant, 660-foot-long continuous block arose along Commonwealth Avenue. This overpowering mass suggests the great early fourteenth-century Palais des Papes at Avignon. The combined elevation achieves an overall effect of a procession of vertical elements through the use of angled piers which separate the window bays. The horizontal bands of these large metal windows, divided by a flat, integrated composition, are almost abstracted-Gothic in feeling. Furthermore, the projecting topmost story and two ground floors frame the recessed intermediate floors to produce a three-dimensional effect. Nothing differen-

tiates this mass save the pointed-arch doorways and the formal, three-bay entrance to Hayden Memorial with its broad flight of stairs.

*#745, THE SCHOOL OF THEOLOGY*, 1947–48, west of the Marsh Plaza, is a smaller version of the main block. A stained-glass window from the original Robinson Chapel (A8) illuminates the hallway. Alongside is *#755, SPEARE HALL*, a two-story wing, headquarters for Metropolitan College. On the other side of the Chapel is *#685, HAYDEN MEMORIAL*. The first section to be constructed, it was rushed to completion in 1939 after M.I.T. sold its downtown Walker building (designed by Fehmer, Tour D), which housed the Boston University School of Management. [The School of Management traces its origin to a 1913 student "More Men Movement." Outnumbered 92 to 27 by female College of Liberal Arts students, male students persuaded the administration to offer evening classes in business to attract "more

*The Palace of the Popes in Avignon, from an eighteenth-century drawing.*

*765–675 Commonwealth Avenue.*

men." The classes were so popular
that by 1916, a new school of business
management remodeled M.I.T.'s
Walker building at 525 Boylston
Street, a block from the then-new College of Liberal Arts (A10). The continuing success of this new school
sustained the university throughout
the Depression.]

In the interior, a foyer, flanked by a
wide series of steps to the classrooms,
leads to the auditorium. Set into the
TERRAZZO floor is the nautical pattern
of a fully rigged ship within a com-
pass, a tribute to the power of Dean
Lord of the School of Management
who, as a boy and man, worked on his
father's sailing ship. He always referred to the foyer as "the main deck."

Golden marble sheathes this hall
and that on the west closest to the
chapel, where heavy bronze doors,
like those on the front, embellish the
entries. Here again, the design commemorates a revered university figure. On the north wall, a large
painted-glass window by Wilbur H.
Burnham depicts Mt. Chocurua, New
Hampshire, which overlooks the be-
loved summer home of William E.
Huntington, president of the university from 1904 to 1911. The top floor
of the classroom block is of a grander
scale. At one time it contained Chenery (D4) Library and exhibition
rooms. The Astronomy Department
and Coit Observatory occupy their
original locations.

*#675, STONE SCIENCE BUILD-
ING,* followed to the east of Hayden
in 1948.

**Across Commonwealth Avenue,
opposite the Main Campus—**

## C4/700 Commonwealth Avenue

1965, Von Storch and Burkavage, Warren
Towers, University dormitory, shops, garage.

Warren Towers commemorates the
"First Family of Boston University."
William Fairfield Warren (1833–1929),
the founder minister of the First
Methodist Church on Bowdoin Street,
had served with the university founders as their pastor and as vice president and managing director of the
Concord Theological Institute. He
was appointed the first president of
Boston University and was largely responsible for building it into a major
institution within five years. His son,
William Marshall Warren (1865–
1953), professor of philosophy, became
dean of the College of Liberal Arts;
and Dean Warren's son, Dr. Shields
Warren (1898–1980), an internationally known pathologist and medical
statesman, served thirty years as a
trustee and as chairman of the board
of trustees of Boston University.

On the building's street facade, a
broad, four-story base supports three
fourteen-story towers. Warren Towers
takes advantage of its commercial site
and provides income from the ground
floor shops and two levels of parking,
shielded by a decorative grid screen.
The ROUGH-AGGREGATE walls with
smooth concrete trim are well suited
to the solid, geometric effect of the IN-
TERNATIONAL style.

Inside, the fourth floor, composed of
large glass windows, runs the full
width of the three towers. It contains
the lounges, dining rooms, laundry,
and games room necessary for a residence for 1,650 students.

*700 Commonwealth Avenue.*

## C5/Park in front of 640–620 Commonwealth Avenue

Unbuilt house sites, platted by Arthur Vinal and Samuel D. Kelley, 1903.

This long strip of land was originally PLATted with driveways leading from the avenue. In 1902, Arthur Vinal and Samuel D. Kelley, architects in the area, filed for permits to build single-family houses. To this day, however, no structures have been erected on the site. This, and the identical land in the next block to the east, were for many years landscaped as parks with flower gardens and wooden post and rail fencing. As the great auto showrooms spread along Commonwealth Avenue, the land changed from the planned residential uses to auto-related trades.

The current park was constructed through the generosity of the Randolph Hearst, Sr., Foundation and alumni trustee Robert Bergenheim. The sculpture relates to the remodeled facade behind it through the use of massive pink-granite blocks. A series of waterfalls and pools create a play of light and sound and, in the winter, ever-changing fantastic ice sculptures.

## C6/640 Commonwealth Avenue

Garage/auto sales room, 1912; remodeled, Richmond and Goldberg, 1956, Boston University School of Public Communication.

The original factory buildings featured a vaguely Tudor Revival facade of red brick and stone trim similar to #620 (C7). The original detail of the simpler, ART DECO–inspired rear elevation can be seen on Cummington Street.

For a million-dollar renovation, the university chose Richmond and Gold-

berg as architects. Both had traveled under the prestigious Rotch Fellowships in 1923 and 1931 and were well versed in the International style. Window shapes and spacing were predetermined by the original buildings. The architects sheathed the industrial facades with pink granite. The projecting central stair tower of glass and black granite also served as a base for the communications antenna.

The building now houses classrooms, and broadcasting and film studios. In 1947, Boston University became the first in the world to offer a degree in Public Relations; three years later, that school consolidated with the School of Communications. In the basement is a remarkable historical and educational resource: 180,000 newspaper clippings dating back to the nineteenth century, donated by the Hearst Corporation when it merged the *Boston Herald* with the *Record-American.*

**Look across Commonwealth Avenue to the left—**

where mixed uses illustrate the uneven development of the Kenmore Square area. To the left of Burger King is a parking lot, the site of a freestanding, Colonial Revival–style mansion that served for a time as the home of the university's president. Double lots neighboring this mansion were purchased at the turn of the century by socially prominent Bostonians, including Henry L. Higginson, but the neighborhood evidently failed to live up to the owners' expectations,

*(Top Right) 640 Commonwealth Avenue.*
*(Bottom Right) 620 Commonwealth Avenue.*

for they never got around to building their proposed mansions. This block contains a wide-ranging mix of several speculator rowhouses, the former Sperry Rand Corporation Building, re-modeled in 1965 into a contemporary-style Boston University School of Nursing, and the former Lahey Clinic (C8), now the School of Education.

## C7/620 Commonwealth Avenue

Auto showroom, Somes and Parsons, 1913;
Boston University Program in Artisanry.

By 1913, the land along Common-wealth Avenue, above Kenmore Square, exhibited an extraordinary proliferation of automobile show-rooms. These buildings (C6, 7, 11, 22, 25) required large expanses of well-lighted garage space and display areas, and floors capable of supporting heavy loads; thus their exterior walls served as functional envelopes delineating the voids between solid supporting piers. Their facades were often embel-lished with vigorous and distinctive designs. At 620, the red-brick orna-mentation is reminiscent of the neigh-boring Tudor Revival structures, but the crisp geometrical pattern of the design, with its emphasis on entrance bays and roofline, recalls the commer-cial purpose of the building by direct-ing attention to the wares within.

## C8/605 Commonwealth Avenue

Lahey Clinic, E. M. Parsons, 1925; later ad-ditions. Boston University School of Educa-tion.

This nationally recognized clinic, since removed to suburban Burling-ton, housed a collective medical prac-tice. As the members of the group

maintained private offices and homes along Bay State Road, they converted the neighborhood from residential to mixed uses (see Tour D).

Over the years, the architects were faced with the problem of setting a large building mass within a smaller-scaled environment. Their solutions divided the structure into two red-brick blocks, four-and-a-half stories high, along Commonwealth Avenue and three stories along Sherborn Street. Sections of varying heights step back from these corner facades al-most unnoticed from the streets. The Federal Revival–style decoration is spare and focuses upon the entrance bay. Here, stone quoins frame the doorway surmounted by a half-round transom. Above is a triple window with limestone pediment. Stone cor-nices and sills give additional form to the discreet composition.

## C9/602 Commonwealth Avenue

Temple Adath Israel, C. H. Blackall, 1903;
Boston University Morse Auditorium.

Morse Auditorium, the second sanc-tuary of Temple Adath Israel, is a sur-vivor of the days when this area was planned for residential use. In 1902, Arthur Vinal had filed building per-mits (C5) for the land next door, ex-pecting to continue his handsome res-idential work from a few blocks away on Bay State Road (D7). When the dis-tinguished Reform Jewish congrega-tion, founded in 1852, purchased the site in 1902, it, therefore, had every reason to believe that its new sanctu-ary would be located in an affluent

---

*(Top Right) 605 Commonwealth Avenue.
(Bottom Right) 602 Commonwealth Ave-nue.*

residential neighborhood. Because congregational participation required an unobstructed view of the podium and fine acoustics, the Temple's trustees selected as architect theatre-designer Clarence Blackhall, the versatile designer of Boston's neo-Baroque Metropolitan Theatre and the chaste, Federal Revival Wilbur and Colonial theatres.

The building is an imposing, marble-sheathed composition of Egyptian and Byzantine styles. Massive, pylon-like CANTED end-bays flank a wide center entrance; a tall weighty cornice frames the facade. The centrality of the dome and the wide entrance, reached by two flights of broad stairs, announce the building's main function as an auditorium. Side elevations are simple, punctuated only by the seven, slender stained-glass windows and their rectangular counterparts in the ground story. A similar design of seven arches on the front facade is now screened by a modern panel. Along the sidewalk, cast-iron posts with chains form a fence; these posts are molded in the same canted shape as the end-bays.

In homage to the current Classical Revival style, Blackhall ornamented the interior foyer and stair halls with classical Greek motifs, most notably in the door transoms, which feature crossed circles within a square. The sanctuary is a dramatic and skillful design characterized by restrained geometry. A shallow, circular dome dominates the square room. Narrow, attenuated parabolic arches house stained-glass windows of predominantly green hues. These shapes repeat again behind the horseshoe-shaped balcony. Great broad arches frame the deep rear balcony and front podium alcoves.

Thus, geometry provides a dignified setting and directs attention to the sacred objects in the ark behind the podium, and on the speakers.

## C10/590 Commonwealth Avenue

Exide Batteries/General Tire Co., 191?; Monosson Building remodeled by John Carl Warnecke, 1983, Boston University Science Center.

Perhaps the most dramatic interior space at the university is the multi-story ATRIUM carved out of a former automobile-related commercial structure. The open white-plastered balconies and red staircases eliminate the traditional segregation of disciplines and encourage the intercommunica-

*The atrium in the Science Center.*

tion of faculty and students. Totally dominating the atrium, two pairs of great ventilator pipes capped by box-like lintels and "jet-engine" forms reach out to each floor level. These blue-green giants create a high-tech aesthetic totally in keeping with the building's purpose.

Stripped of its typical three-bay, triple-window covering, the former commercial space produced a versatile steel frame for the stark brick Commonwealth Avenue front. Although the new facade is severe and geometrical, the red-brick materials, white-limestone window sills, and column/lintel forms allude to the Classical Re-

*Architect's model showing projected park space in front of new Science Center, with proposed Cummington Street mall.*

vival buildings of the neighborhood (Tours B, D). The absence of windows at the top level creates a heavy, horizontal entablature/lintel effect.

The strips of windows, full height at ground level, single above, wrap around the building and integrate the elevations, one story higher. By framing the entrance at #592, the architects wisely focused upon the drama of the tall, narrow atrium.

**Turn right onto Cummington Street.**

## C11/Cummington Mall

An early attempt to develop town-houses at #8–12 and 65–71 faltered; #12 was soon converted to an animal

hospital. Cummington became a typical Boston back alley bordering railroad tracks, with stables (C13, 14) and, later, garages. During this transition period, the unbuilt lots constantly changed owners until the mid-teens when automobile-related commercial buildings imposed their use on the sites. Note the design of the rear facades of these structures. These architects were often well trained but limited by the budget and needs of their clients. Benjamin Fox, for example, architect of #64, also designed the apartment house at 500 Park Drive (B27) and a downtown hotel.

In 1983–84, Boston University tripled its science and engineering facilities. Cummington Street was converted to a tree-lined mall, its collection of facades integrated by yellow entryways sporting bright, university-red doors. On the vacant lot between the Biology Building (#2) and the Science and Engineering Lab (#28), the university has erected the contemporary-style Nickelodeon Theatre. Its five auditoria vary in size from 86 seats to 412. Used as science lecture halls in the morning, they convert to income-producing rented movie theatres in the afternoons and evenings.

## C12/111 Cummington Street

Somes and Parsons, automobile showroom and garage, 1909; now University science classrooms and Academic Computing Center.

The builders of moderate-cost commercial structures were not always indifferent to aesthetic considerations, as these buildings demonstrate. Geometric motifs, inspired by Art Deco, could be readily applied to poured con-

crete, allowing the architects to introduce an avant-garde, machine-age tone into their designs. Typical are the LOW-RELIEF receding planes that form the enframement for the metal windows. The angular composition has a vertical emphasis that breaks up the wide, 547-foot facade.

A shallow pediment and recessed horizontal panel crown each group of three bays. The 50' by 60' high end wall is also composed of a strong vertical/horizontal grid. Brick, laid at right angles to the windows and in a wide panel beneath, creates a stylish entrance. Three rows of bricks in a diamond pattern centered between the floors integrate the wall vertically.

Thus, the architects accepted the utilitarian purpose of this building, solved the functional problems, and created an appropriate aesthetic style in a new material: concrete.

## C13/110 Cummington Street

A. S. Desko, 1899; boarding stables of Henry Turner, garage; 1963, Boston University College of Engineering.

In a commanding position at the head of the street, this building illustrates New England factory architecture of the nineteenth and early twentieth centuries. Although the Lawrence trustees (Tour B) did not sell this land until 1899, the building's style incorporates Queen Anne Revival motifs. Industrial buildings tended to be functional, economical, and thus conservative. In 1963, the first floor was al-

---

*(Top Right) 111 Cummington Street.*
*(Bottom Right) Pediment, 110 Cummington Street.*

tered to meet the requirements of the College of Engineering, which moved from quarters alongside Logan Airport in East Boston. Twenty years later, in 1983–84, the University renovated the interior and doubled the space with a large addition to the rear, along Babbitt Street.

The twelve-bay, four-story, red-brick facade is a fine symmetrical composition. Subtle changes in window treatment give character to the building without unprofitable expense: second- and third-floor openings are segmental, while those on the fourth floor are rectangular, their shape emphasized by strong stone lintels. The only other ornamentation is the stepped corbel brick cornice and central triangular pediment enclosing a medallion and flanked by end piers. The two-bay roof addition is later.

This building, along with an earlier small structure attached to the right, was part of the stable business of Henry C. Turner (C14).

## C14/112 Cummington Street

Horse-shoeing shop of Henry C. Turner, 1900; 1909 and 1923, rebuilt by Samuel D. Kelley; 1963, Boston University College of Engineering.

A member of the black Boston business community, Henry C. Turner (1852–1919), erected the first structure on this site. Turner earlier operated a stable and horse-shoeing business on Northampton Street in the new South End. As residential areas expanded, Turner moved his business, first to Cambria Street and then here to Lawton (later renamed Cummington) Street, where he leased the large premises at #110 (C13).

In 1900, Turner applied for a permit to build a shoeing shop on this site. The shop was faced with a metal front, probably similar to the one here today, and measured 25'6" wide by 45' deep; it was one story (13') high with a flat roof. An invoice from the first decade of the century illustrates Turner's ability to keep up with the times: horses are still stabled but are now "clipped by electric power." Furthermore, the enterprising Turner also added "auto storage and care" to his services.

In 1909, a new owner, the trustees for the C. E. Cotting estate, with Samuel D. Kelley, architect, filed a permit to build a larger structure, flush with the rear of #110, twice as deep and three feet higher. Then in 1923, Kelley demolished this 1909 structure and rebuilt on the same foundations a two-story building 28 feet high and five feet deeper (95 feet). Its Colonial Revival features are, in fact, a covering of inexpensive PRESSED galvanized iron. Classical pilasters and panels enframe the two-bay first story. On the second story, columns with elaborate capitals form a five-part cornice. This machine-made, prefabricated decoration is repeated along the alley facade of nine bays.

**Look left along Babbitt Street to the 1983 extension of the College of Engineering, which filled in an empty parking lot, as did the new Nickelodeon Theatre.**

**Walk to Commonwealth Avenue and turn left.**

*110–112 Cummington Street.*

## C15/708–714 Commonwealth Avenue

Rowhouses, J. P. Neal, 1875; commercial. 710 and 712 privately owned.

Although now a garish four-unit commercial strip, this group is historically important as the first set of rowhouses built in the area. They represent the typical work of the VERNACULAR builder/architect active in Boston in the last quarter of the nineteenth century. The land had been part of the Lawrence family's Cottage Farm development in Brookline (Tour B). Among the Lawrence family homes were two houses at the end of this block, along St. Mary's Street. An

1875 atlas shows the land belonging to James P. Neal, who had planned four identical brick-and-brownstone, mansard-roofed one-family houses.

Number 708, owned by the university, is drastically altered, but its original appearance can be reconstructed by comparing features from the four identical units. The high steps attest to the frequent flooding from the tidal Charles River, which came under control only with the construction of storm sewers in 1884. Thus all the later buildings on Tours C and D could safely build ground-level entrances.

Ornament is playful and varied outside, spare within, indicating housing

*708–714 Commonwealth Avenue.*

for average-income families. Rosettes embellish the triangular pediments over the second-floor entrance. To the left is a three-sided bay with brown-stone lintels. A decorative recessed brick cross-motif acts as a belt cornice between the two floors. At the eaves, a cornice of pressed brick combines the Queen Anne elements of stepped CORBELS and dentil molding. At the mansard roof level, wooden decorative pilasters and brackets support the cornices of the dormer windows. Project-ing sawn scrolls along the side frames draw attention to the single window above the door bay.

Interior decoration is minimal. The staircase spindles combine rounded turnings with squared sections. The posts at each stage terminate in round discs.

## C16/The Sert Master Plan

1961–66.

In the 1950s, the thirty-year-old mas-ter plan finally reached completion. Ever-increasing enrollment over-whelmed the postwar Charles River Campus, while classrooms and librar-ies remained scattered all over the City of Boston. This newest plan, drawn up by José Luis Sert, Dean of the Harvard Graduate School of De-sign, along with his associates, Profes-sors Jackson and Gourley, accom-plished three goals. First, Sert reoriented the campus toward the river, reaffirming Cram's riverside concept and creating a major land-mark along the Charles River Basin; secondly, the high-rise composition visually linked the site, downriver, to

98

the new City of Boston and, upriver, to the Harvard campus, with Sert's high-rise Peabody Terrace and Holyoke Center. Thirdly, he created a vertical academic enclave which shelters spacious courtyards and pedestrian ways.

Fortunately, none of the new buildings dominate the frail, Gothic Marsh Chapel (C2) which continues to form the center of the campus. Structural elements are stressed rather than masked, while MODULOR proportions provide a human scale, reflecting the influence of Sert's master, the French architect, Le Corbusier. Although the Law School and Law Library (C17), Student Union and Mugar Library (C20) all share common materials and vocabulary, each building still illustrates a distinctive shape and idiom. Massed together with existing Cram buildings, they provide variety and balance.

**Look up to the left of the chapel toward the high-rise School of Law—then pass through the arcade at the left of the chapel.**

## C17/765–67 Commonwealth Avenue

School of Law and Law Library, Sert, Jackson and Gourley, 1961.

The Law School made its move here in 1961 from its downtown quarters on Beacon Hill at 11 Ashburton Place (A10). The School of Education shared the tower until its move in 1980 to 605 Commonwealth Avenue (C8).

Massive, vertical groupings of window bays nineteen stories tall and the giant flue of the central heating plant thrust upward to meet the rooftop service towers. The lower floors relate to the neighboring buildings and the *JAPANESE GARDEN* while, at the same time, acting as a base for the tower. Here the interplay of horizontal and vertical white window frames, reddish-blue brick, and blue metal panels repeats the modules on the adjoining Law Library.

*THE PAPPAS LAW LIBRARY* is distinguished by large, quarter-round CLERESTORY structures which echo the pointed arches of the nearby chapel arcade and the neo-Gothic windows of the chapel.

In the interior, the gray concrete walls display the imprint of the wooden molds, which were constructed to form angled patterns. The model courtroom is paneled in blond oak; the Moot Court is decorated in purple fabric, the color associated with the law degree.

**Climb the stairs to the terrace west of the Law School to view the river.**

## C18/North Bank of Charles River, The University Boathouse

Walter Kattelle, for the Metropolitan District Commission, 1909.

Boathouses have always been focal points along riverscapes. Harvard University had enlivened the Charles River with a wooden boathouse as early as 1890, replacing it with Weld Boathouse in the new Queen Anne Revival style in 1907. Designed by the firm of Peabody and Stearn, Weld serves as a stylish companion to the architects' 1900 Classical Revival-style Newall Boathouse opposite, alongside the Boylston Street Bridge. In 1909, the Metropolitan District

*Sert site plan for the Schools of Law and
Education, 1963. (From New Architecture
in Boston, 1965)*

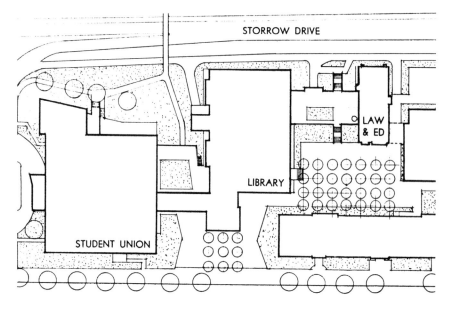

STORROW DRIVE

LAW
& ED

LIBRARY

STUDENT UNION

**SITE PLAN**

*(Right) Commonwealth Avenue towers from
across the Charles.*

*The Boston University Boathouse. (Boston University Photo Services)*

Commission, sensitive to the prominence of these Harvard boathouses at the bend of the newly-embanked Charles River, produced this down-river Colonial Revival design to high standards.

The function determined the form. Specifications called for "the best quality bronze fittings, clear pine, double hung windows and green slate roof." One-and-a-half-story boat-bays flank the symmetrical, three-bay, two-story central portion. The lower level serves as boat storage. Here, three bright red double doors, wide enough for the boats, are set within segmental openings with keystone centered on the frame. The second story is divided into rooms. Here, the window pattern alternates two-over-one windows with triple six-over-one. The eyebrow window centered in the gable-on-hip roof adds a note of gaiety and sport to

the design. These details contribute to a symmetrical, chaste, and fashionable design.

**Return to the Japanese Garden and turn right.**

## C19/771 Commonwealth Avenue, Mugar Memorial Library

Sert, Jackson and Gourley, 1966.

Mugar Library is the intellectual center of the university. Within this new building, the university consolidated nine separate libraries scattered throughout the campus. In the tradition of the founders, Claflin, Rich, and Sleeper, the donor, Stephen Mugar, has stated that this library:

> . . . was like a debt I have contracted for and one which I am happy and delighted to be able to pay. Coming to America many years ago from Armenia, I have never taken for granted all the wonderful things this country has to offer.

*The Mugar Memorial Library.*

The library's sculptural mass and step-like profile dominate the view from the river. It is an energetic composition of concrete, glass, and red-glazed panels shaped into bays, recesses, balconies, and service towers. The architects used the facade as a canvas on which to create an abstract painting, with windows as the dominant shapes. The street facade balances a two-story glass entry with the upper fifth-floor BRISE DE SOLEIL, a sun screen, projecting and shielding four-part window clusters. The upper sto-ries feature symmetrical rows of narrow windows.

In the interior, the rich red wool carpet is a foil for plaster walls in primary colors and the red-brick walls POINTED with charcoal-colored mortar. Furniture is broad and massive in pale oak, ash, and birch. The MODULAR design allows for open floor space; the first three floors serve as open study and reference areas. The fifth floor, Chenery Library, houses the Special Collections, an extensive repository for manuscripts and artifacts relating to such diverse subjects as theatre arts, Robert Frost, Abraham Lincoln, and

Black America. Here, a large exhibition room displays these treasures on a rotating basis. Additional exhibition spaces for these collections flank the ground-floor entrance.

## C20/775 Commonwealth Avenue

The Link and George Sherman Union, Sert, Jackson and Gourley, 1963.

Integrating the Marsh Plaza and the Student Union is the Link, a seventy-foot-high glass inner courtyard. As the route to the cafeteria, it is a popular meeting area, replacing the famous

Marble (A11) of the Copley Square campus. An information area and bank serve as the entry unit, while a grand staircase leads to the varied activities of the Student Union above.

The Student Union is the social center of the campus. The complex contains a cafeteria, game rooms, meeting rooms, post office, lounges, and a ballroom. The rear tower provides space for student organizations, offices, and a faculty-staff dining room.

The four-story facade on Commonwealth Avenue maintains the street scale while a higher, six-story, more massive rear wing repeats the form. The two wings join at the center in a stairstep fashion which echoes the ad-

*The George Sherman Union.*

jacent library. This profile is emphasized on the west facade by a similar stairstep placement of one window per floor. The buildings alternate dark gray brick with horizontal light concrete bands which divide floor levels and frame balconies and parapets in much the same way that the belt and roof cornices in classical vocabulary function along Bay State Road (Tour D). Thus, Sert anchors the western end of the old campus by paying homage to eastern Bay State Road. Sert also refers to the Castle (D4) and the Armory (C27) in the service towers.

The distinguishing ornamental feature of the Union building is the concrete *brise de soleil* which screens the front facade. Four-story glass bays divide this screen into end bays and a broad central bay. Along the top floors of the rear section, the street facade continues as a variation on the screen which so strongly dominates the front.

## C21/785 Commonwealth Avenue (University Road)

Shell Oil Building, Gilbert Miles Ramsey, 1931; Boston University Sargent College of Allied Health Professions.

This site has a storied past. A British fort here, at the foot of Essex Street, was the center of the only battle fought in the Town of Brookline during the Revolution; while just to the west, in Brighton, a large stockyard held cattle for Washington's troops at Dorchester. In 1821 a milldam, topped by a toll road, joined the markets of Boston with the gardens and slaughterhouses of Brighton; by 1855 a commuter rail station had opened across the avenue at Cottage Farm; and a year later, a bridge at this site replaced the historic Cottage Farm Ferry. Between 1882 and 1890, the flats were filled in, and the Cousens Brothers opened a coalyard. They continued to expand their wharf area with gravel fill over the next thirty years. In 1925, a plan was unveiled to erect a luxury hotel and yacht marina on the coal-

*785 Commonwealth Avenue.*

yard site. The twelve- to fourteen-story structure was to contain an assortment of smart shops and a terrace where orchestras would serenade the guests during dining hours. To the undoubted relief of the owners of the newly-launched Sheraton and Myles Standish apartment hotels on nearby Bay State Road (D22 and D31), this ambitious project was never brought to fruition. In 1929, a year after the construction of the present steel-frame Cottage Farm Bridge (now Boston University Bridge), the General Tire and Rubber Company Retirement Fund purchased the site as an investment property; and two years later, Gilbert Miles Ramsey designed the Art Deco–style structure that stands here today. The building served as the New England headquarters of the Shell Oil Company before being bought by Boston University in 1951. It was then occupied by the College of General Education until 1958, when it became the new home of Sargent College.

(Sargent College was founded by Dudley Allen Sargent, M.D., a former circus performer and acrobat, and an early advocate of "physical fitness for all." In 1879, Sargent was invited to establish a program at Harvard; through subsequent reorganization, growth, and mergers, the Sargent School established itself in Cambridge. In 1929, the school became affiliated with Boston University, and by 1934 was able to offer a four-year degree program in physical education.)

The three-story, reinforced concrete building has a crisp, linear composition, with fluted pilasters and narrow horizontal bands. The elaborate cast-stone FRIEZE depicts marine themes, and the shells which crown the pilasters are mementos of its original ten-

ant. The huge neon sign which originally embellished the roof can now be seen on Memorial Drive, across the river in Cambridge.

**West of the bridge and across Commonwealth Avenue, note:**

## C22/808 Commonwealth Avenue

Fuller Cadillac automobile showroom, Albert Kahn, 1928; University-owned.

The imposing size and choice location of this building were intended to convey an impression of opulence and confidence—befitting the dealership of a top-of-the-line luxury car. Such showroom buildings were commissioned by automobile companies from nationally-known architects. Albert

*808 Commonwealth Avenue.*

Kahn, self-taught architect of international stature, designed for practically all the auto firms in America. An exponent of organizational efficiency and master of concrete, he was among the first to perceive the importance of improving the design of factory and industrial buildings.

Expensive limestone and marble sheathe the huge seven-bay, five-story-high corner structure. Classical motifs appear in a restrained and almost modern effect. On the exterior, shallow fluted pilasters and triple windows form an integrated composition with horizontal elements: the spandrels between the windows on the top three floors, the wide bands framing the second story, and the broad roof parapet. In place of the traditional CAPITAL at the top of the pilaster sits a rosette, perhaps emblematic of a wheel.

The interior employs this classical vocabulary in a luxurious fashion. Terrazzo floors alternate hexagonal and diamond sections. Each massive, hexagonal column is capped with gilded moldings and foliage. The ceiling, echoing the floor, alternates gilded hexagonal coffers with medallions set in squares.

Because of its great size and expense, this building was known as "Fuller's Folly." Alvan T. Fuller, the proprietor of the dealership, served as governor of Massachusetts during the notorious Sacco-Vanzetti trial in 1927, the year before the building was erected.

**Continue west, on the river side of Commonwealth Avenue.**

## C23/Topographical History of the West Campus

In 1870, the City of Boston annexed Brighton, along with a strip of land in Brookline (from Essex Street along Commonwealth Avenue) that connected Brighton to Brookline. (In later years, residents referred to this strip as the "Polish Corridor," alluding to the post-World War I settlement which ceded a strip of Prussia to landlocked Poland.)

On the right, approaching the School for the Arts, a small park borders the intersection of the bridge, railroad tracks, and Massachusetts Turnpike. This green spot is all that remains of a vast river meadow to the west and north. By 1890, Eben Jordan had converted this drained marshland (2,784,756 square feet) into Beacon Park, complete with hotel and grandstands from which the Boston Driving and Athletic Association could watch the horses and carriages of the gentry.

West of this tract lay the Cottage Farm properties of architect George M. Dexter (Tour B) which originally reached to these water meadows and were part of the Town of Brookline. According to the 1909 atlas, one Gordon Dexter had purchased 500,940 square feet of land east of Malvern Street from the Edward D. Sohier estate. A vestige of this farmland still survives in the university's Malvern Street athletic field.

At the turn of the century, Charles Francis Adams II, having successfully developed the lower two blocks of Bay State Road (Tour D), purchased this large tract just west of the bridge. The site, however, did not become a residential neighborhood but, instead, became by default (and probably with financial loss to the Adamses) the

Allston Golf Club. It is on this golf course land that tour stops numbered C25–C29 are now located.

**Also on south side of Commonwealth Avenue—**

## C24/830–844 Commonwealth Avenue

Norcross Brothers for M. Rudnick, auto showroom, 1920; now stores.

A few developers specialized in speculative commercial showroom construction. The high turnover of this type of property required simple flexible interior spaces which could be subdivided as needed. During the halcyon days of auto sales, there was little risk to the real-estate investor.

Here materials are of modest quality such as poured or cast concrete and wood. Colonial Revival details add an air of affluent style, reflecting the adjacent residential neighborhoods. Flat pilasters joined by narrow lintels and a closed roofline parapet define each individual showroom while integrating the six-part composition.

Ornament concentrates around the narrow entrance bays where a small but lavish arrangement of Ionic columns supports an entablature and modillion cornice surmounted by a swagged SWANS' NECK BROKEN-PEDIMENT with urn. Acting on the theory that more is better, the designer then added a high keystone lintel and, above that, another triangular pediment/gable at the roofline. While these costly details entice the customer into the showroom, they fail to integrate an overall design.

**On the north side of Commonwealth Avenue beyond the small park—**

## C25/855 Commonwealth Avenue

Arthur Bowditch, Admiral Building for Noyes Buick, 1919; Boston University School for the Arts.

This high-style, PERPENDICULAR GOTHIC commercial building is but one of many styles in which Arthur Bowditch worked successfully

*830 Commonwealth Avenue.*

*855 Commonwealth Avenue.*

throughout the university neighborhood. The huge structure has been adapted by the School for the Arts into studios, galleries, and areas for practice and performance.

The precision of detail and the harmonious proportions of the well-dressed stones create an austere, refined facade. On the street elevation, flat pilasters divide multiple windows into eleven bays, each crowned with a flat, crenellated lintel. The corner and center bays define the shape with two instead of three windows. Along the high ground floor, these bays form an arcade of Tudor arches whose moldings are punctuated by carved rosettes. Between each arch is a carved panel with heraldic shield below from which projects a copper wall lantern with trefoil MULLIONS. A series of arches frames the recessed center

door; stone blocks now fill in the remaining arches.

The main showrooms now serve as a gallery and rehearsal areas. Both are

*Auto mechanics update traditional motifs on classical capitals in the Boston University Gallery, 855 Commonwealth Avenue.*

109

Another example of new uses for old buildings, is the seven-story structure at 881 Commonwealth av., near the Commonwealth Armory, a turn-of-the-century building that architects and engineers Symmes, Maini, & McKee, of Cambridge, renovated for Boston Univer-sity. The run-down building, which proved to be structurally sound, got a new skin of porcelain enamel panels and bronze tinted glass. Old columns were left intact but refinished with a waterproof epoxy. The structure serves as an administration center for BU.

*From the* Boston Sunday Globe, *July 21, 1974.*

entered from the rear down a short flight of wide steps. Powerful, dramatic Gothic piers support a shallow-ribbed, vaulted ceiling. The capitals are deeply undercut with fruit and naturalistic foliage, but in place of corner volutes, twentieth-century auto-mechanics surprisingly usurp the role of traditional medieval figures.

The east corner showroom originally served the university as a student lounge, but the windows are now sealed off and this large space is used for theatre rehearsals.

Here a great Tudor-arched fireplace with an overmantel of three trefoil arches encloses a clock with leaf ornament. To the side of the entrance, the grand staircase rises majestically, its balustrade of pierced trefoil arches and heavy molded rail anchored by a

square carved newel post crowned with a heraldic shield. As in other great mansions of this period (D4, 15), the staircase divides, then reverses at the top to form a second-floor balcony, now sealed off.

## C26/881 Commonwealth Avenue

*The Youth's Companion* printing plant, 1917; 1974, remodeled into University offices, Symmes, Maini and McKee; 1982, new rear addition.

The modern renovation masks the buildings' distinguished origins. It was erected as a printing plant for *The Youth's Companion*, the first American weekly paper for children which, by the 1880s, had the largest circulation of any literary paper in the world.

The magazine's owners consistently indulged in high-style architectural patronage. Their first quarters were at 41 Temple Place, a Second Empire–style building designed by Nathaniel Bradlee in 1869 and now a designated Boston landmark (it survived the fire of 1872). The firm next commissioned Hartwell and Richardson, who produced the large red-brick and brownstone, Romanesque Revival–style plant which dominates the corner of Berkeley Street and Columbus Avenue.

*The Youth's Companion*'s new 1917 Tudor Revival–style building concentrated ornament on the four corners, suggesting the central entrance-gate tower that is basic to this style. Copying the Armory (C27), the towers feature shallow arches, broad-banded WATERSTRUCK-BRICK-and-limestone entrances, and mock battlements at the roof line.

In 1975, the university renovated the printing plant to provide office space. The architects retained the original well-balanced design of horizontal and vertical elements framing large windows. The exterior piers remained intact but were covered with a waterproof epoxy, while the original windows were replaced by bronze-tinted glass. Beneath the windows and along the roofline, porcelain enamel panels now cover the castle-like crenellations. In conversion, the structure has lost its initial stylistic identity which related it so effectively to the nearby Massachusetts Armory.

The walkway connecting the building to the three-story structure behind it was added in 1982.

## C27/925 Commonwealth Avenue

Armory of the Massachusetts Division of the National Guard, James McLaughlin, 1916.

Here, at last, the castle-like Tudor Revival style is used in a genuinely martial setting. James E. McLaughlin, the architect of the Boston Latin School, faced special requirements in the design for the local cavalry division. The broad set-back and entrance bridge at the third level provide space for a moat-like ramp servicing the two levels below. Wagons would load feed for the horses from railroad cars at the rear of the building and then roll up into the first and second levels along special ramps. The land to the east served as an open drill ground for the cavalry; it was later covered by the present three-story additions.

The theatrical approach is through iron gates hung on open-grille posts attached to great brick-and-limestone piers. A bridge then leads over the moat/driveway to a massive three-story gatehouse. Projecting, two-story "guardhouses" flank the doorway. McLaughlin lavishly applied a Tudor Revival vocabulary of blind trefoil arches, heraldic shields, powerful buttresses, and alternating bands of red waterstruck brick and white limestone. A crenellated parapet completes the image of a fortified castle.

The armory was immediately the dominant building on the streetscape. Within a year, the owners of *The Youth's Companion*, well-known for their architectural sophistication, constructed their new printing plant in stylistic homage to the Armory (C26).

**Turn right onto Gaffney Street.**

*925 Commonwealth Avenue.*

## C28/32 Gaffney Street

Gatehouse of Boston Braves baseball field, 1915; University police/daycare center.

In designing their gatehouse, the Boston Braves baseball club (C29) chose the new MISSION REVIVAL style, which reflected the Spanish Colonial tradition. Two years later, this would be popularized at the 1915 Panama-Pacific Exposition in San Diego, California. The two-and-a-half-story gatehouse features stucco walls and a sloping tile roof with exposed rafters. The arcaded ground floor served as the admission gates. While the center bays are now enclosed, the open side bays still lead to the grandstand and the West Campus courtyard.

A simple brick string-course in dentil pattern separates the ground-floor arcade from the second-floor one-over-one windows. The three-part composition emphasizes stepped third-story wall-gable wings flanking the center sloping-tile roof with its two hipped dormers. Windows on this level are grouped in threes and feature an unusual mullion pattern.

**Walk through the gate house to the back of the building. Note the exact repetition of the front facade in the third-floor rear design.**

## C29/Nickerson Field

1915 Braves Field; 1954, Boston University
athletic field.

Not many college athletes can claim
to play in the footsteps of a major
professional team. The present Nickerson Field was the home of the Boston Braves, the National League baseball team from 1915 to 1953. In 1928,
Boston University located its sports
activities at the first Nickerson Field
in a meadow alongside the Charles
River in Weston, a thirty-minute train
ride from the Copley Square Campus
in Boston. Rumor has it that not a few
college athletes acquired their spend-
ing money by refunding their train
tickets and hitchhiking to practice instead.

Land-taking by the Massachusetts
Turnpike Authority (C23) coincided
with the Boston Braves' move to Mil-

waukee in the early 1950s, and a deal
was struck with the university. Grass
two feet high was mowed, the grandstand was torn down, and the playing
field relocated. The first-base pavilion
and sidelines remained. The field now
serves primarily for student athletics,
community and professional teams,
and for the annual commencement
ceremonies.

## C30/Courtyard

272–275 Babcock Street

The courtyard inside the gatehouse
leads alongside the grandstand to the
West Campus dormitories and is
framed by a series of walls. The landscaping and materials skillfully integrate the disparate elements of grandstand and dormitories. The walls
repeat the salmon brick of the towers.

*32 Gaffney Street.*

*Cheerleaders on Nickerson Field, with Claflin, Sleeper, and Rich Halls in the background. (Boston University Photo Services)*

The shallow curves, pierced by small square openings faced with projecting concrete blocks alternate with narrow concrete panels. A lattice of small, open square tiles screens the grandstand behind. Benches and plantings provide terrace space for the dormitories beyond (C31).

## C31/273–275 Babcock Street

Claflin, Sleeper, and Rich Halls, Searle, Von Storch and Steffian, 1963–64, University dormitories.

Placed in an arc facing the athletic field are three interrelated twelve-story, Contemporary-style, slab structures. On the narrow brick ends, a single vertical band of double windows rises up the center bay. The long fa-cades are composed entirely of windows set in a narrow concrete grid with horizontal spandrels in a brick basketweave pattern. On the ground floor, living and dining areas are walled with a honeycomb pattern of cast concrete squares enclosing a variety of window spaces. The upper floors look out onto Nickerson Field and offer a panoramic view of the Charles River with Cambridge to the left and the City of Boston to the right.

*Tour D*

# The Bay State Road Local Historic District

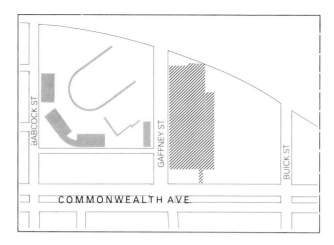

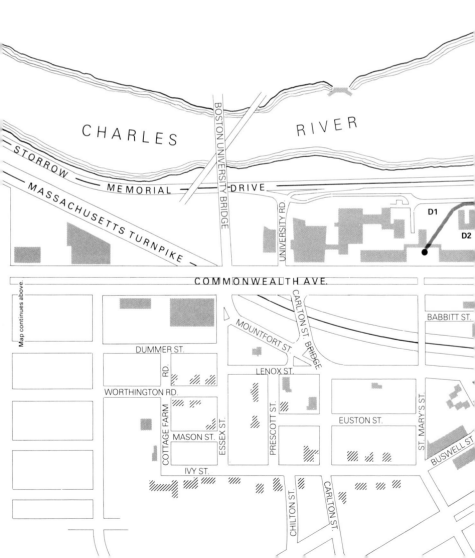

## Tour D  The Bay State Road Local Historic District

D1  Warren Alpert Mall
D2  264–270 Bay State Road
D3  233 Bay State Road, Hillel House
D4  225 Bay State Road, The Castle
D5a  Trachtenberg Park
D5b  211 Bay State Road
D6  214–208 Bay State Road
D7  211–201 Bay State Road
D8  191 Bay State Road, Harriet Richards House
D9  179–171 Bay State Road

D10  167–169 Bay State Road
D11  168 Bay State Road
D12  157 Bay State Road
D13  153 Bay State Road
D14  152 Bay State Road
D15  147 Bay State Road, Dunn House
D16  145–143 Bay State Road
D17  141 Bay State Road
D18a  125 Bay State Road
D18b  121 Bay State Road, Admissions
D19  128 Bay State Road
D20  110–118 Bay State Road
D21  55 Deerfield Street

D22  91 Bay State Road, Shelton Hall
D23  83 Bay State Road
D24  81 Bay State Road
D25  73 Bay State Road
D26  71–69 Bay State Road
D27  67 Bay State Road
D28  61–59 Bay State Road
D29  2 Raleigh Street
D30  1 Raleigh Street
D31  30 Bay State Road, Myles Standish Hall
D32  632 Beacon Street, Myles Standish Annex
D33  660 Beacon Street, University Bookstore
D34  Kenmore Square

● Starting Point of Tour
■ Ending Point of Tour

▶▪ Walking Tour
▨ University Properties

▨ Privately Owned Properties

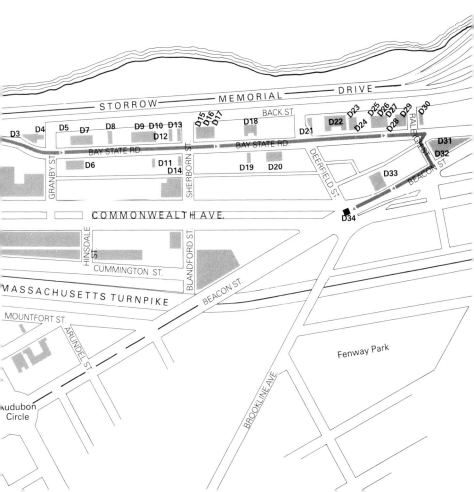

*Second Harrison Gray Otis House, 85 Mt. Vernon Street, 1802: an influential model for later Back Bay homes.*

In spite of stylistic variations, the houses along Bay State Road bear a distinct family resemblance. This is because they were, for the most part, built within a relatively short span of time (between 1890 and 1915) and for a particular segment of the population: upper- and middle-class professionals.

The two-and-a-half decades preceding the Great War were a period of affluence and of common belief in the virtues of tradition. In choosing designs for their new Bay State Road homes, the owners sought to recapture the quiet elegance of Beacon Hill. The Classical Revival form, particularly its Federal Revival variant, predominates, offering a uniform streetscape of brick rowhouses, discreetly trimmed in stone and wood, in a Greek or Roman manner. The swelling BOWFRONTS, elaborate fanlights, and transoms hint of the opulence within.

A number of the city's leading architects—Arthur Little, Arthur Vinal, Edmund Wheelwright, and William Y. Peters—purchased lots on Bay State Road and built houses for themselves and their clients, endowing the neighborhood with a gently "artistic" flavor (reminiscent of Tite Street in London's Chelsea). Boston "Brahmins," with such names as Forbes, Saltonstall, and Weld, lived alongside professionals such as Dr. Elliott Joslin, famous for his pioneering treatment of diabetes. This fashionable clientele demanded a sophisticated level of craftsmanship and tempered their conservatism with an appreciation of the latest continental design motifs. Other dwellings, constructed for clients of moderate means or for open-market speculation, were simply scaled-down versions of their more imposing neighbors.

With the advent of the automobile, the neighborhood's residential character underwent a change. The affluent emigrated to homes in the suburbs; apartment houses appeared on the few remaining lots, and mansions and townhouses were divided into doctors' offices or apartments. In recent years, the story of Bay State Road (now a LOCAL HISTORIC DISTRICT) is that of its growing association with Boston University and its gradual absorption into the university's Charles River Campus.

**Tour D starts at Marsh Plaza. Pass through arcade on the right into—**

## D1/Warren Alpert Mall

1970

This open space is all that remains of Cram's plan for a riverview campus. Boston University had actually filled in the tidal flats for a 1600-foot-wide river terrace when the City of Boston seized the land by eminent domain in 1929 for the Storrow Memorial Park, and thereby separated the campus from the Charles. Of a series of connected quadrangles facing a waterfront park, only the southern facades on Commonwealth Avenue sides were constructed.

This landscaped site forms a meeting and recreation area. It integrates the pre-existing Classical Revival–style apartment buildings along Bay State Road on the east with the contemporary high-rise 1960s campus opposite and the great, neo-Gothic academic block between.

**Turn east and continue along Bay State Road.**

## D2/270–264 Bay State Road

Apartment house, Frank Wilcox, 1913; academic departments.

Apartment buildings of this type were based on a style originating in Paris and introduced into Boston in mid-nineteenth century. Known locally as "FRENCH FLATS," their Gallic origins evidently endowed them with a somewhat risqué aura, reinforced by the fact that their inhabitants were obliged to share a common entrance lobby, denoting a degree of intimacy rare in middle-class housing.

This building was one of the few structures standing on the west end of Bay State Road when the university acquired the area in 1920. The flight to the suburbs had already begun, and this speculator apartment had already changed hands three times since its construction seven years earlier.

Evidence of its decline can be found in a report to the new owner, Boston University, from the former building manager:

> I practically finished the buildings. This property was in very poor condition as regards the . . . property and tenants. It is now . . . first class.

The pair of five-and-a-half-story yellow-brick-and-limestone apartment houses adjoin in a narrow U-shape. On the street ends, hexagonal bays balance the inner half-round bays, which artfully turn the corner into a courtyard. Colonial Revival limestone details sheathe the ground and top floors and embellish the windows and entrances. Prominent stone quoins, frames with keystone, and fluted friezes decorated with vertical ropes of foliage enframe the first-floor windows. Stained-glass window transoms add additional touches of luxury.

The elaborate one-and-a-half-story porticoed entrances mirror each other across the narrow courtyard. Richly detailed wooden pilasters separate the arched glass entry, divided into three Palladian-like sections which are repeated on the interior.

## D3/233 Bay State Road

Hillel House, Krokyn and Browne, 1953. Private.

Like the prow of a great ship, Hillel House looms above Alpert Mall. Built

*Courtyard, 264–270 Bay State Road.*

in the International style, it acts as a foil to the Gothic-style Castle behind (D4). The four-story vertical stairwell-window defines the separation of the two structures. On the street facade, the middle two-story checkerboard band of smooth limestone hangs suspended between windows, setting up a dynamic interaction with the surrounding space. The rounded "prow" end seems to thrust outward from the ground floor band of glass below and open balcony above.

A triangular entry-well deep in the wall draws the visitor past a strip of office windows and through the glass doors. On the bottom and top levels, a band of narrow vertical windows to the left echoes the stairwell shaft. Flagstone in shades of gray and violet further emphasizes the smooth surfaces of the middle checkerboard wall. Along the river facade, large glass windows bring inside the spectacular view, thus extending the interior space.

Within, durable materials of flagstone, terrazzo, and blond oak panels have enabled the original design to survive thirty years of use as a student center. Lounges, dining facilities, seminar rooms, and a small chapel open off a dramatic four-story oval stairwell at the wide end of the building.

## D4/225 Bay State Road

Lindsay Mansion, Chapman and Frazer with George Bosworth, 1905; the Castle, administration offices.

If ever a house reflected its owner's personality, it is this picturesque Tudor Revival mansion. Its owner, William Lindsay (1858–1922), was a prominent Boston businessman and *littérateur,* who strove for a Gothic effect in some of his writings, such as *The Severed Mantle,* "A Romance of Medieval Provence," and *The Wine of Rousillon,* a blank-verse drama set in France in the Middle Ages.

Its second owner, Oakes Ames, abandoned his lavish, French-chateau-style mansion (by Fehmer and Page) at the corner of Massachusetts and Commonwealth Avenues in the Back Bay to join in the exodus to Bay State Road. In 1939, at the end of the Great Depression, Boston University purchased the property for the amount of the back taxes owed to the city—the funds being donated jointly by Oakes Ames and University Trustee Dr. William Chenery. Serving first as the president's home, it now houses offices and is used for social activities. Its lavish rooms are well suited to receptions and small conferences, while the ground level serves as a popular English-style pub.

The L-shaped, four-story mansion appears to be a free-standing house, since the road curves here toward the river, concealing the adjacent Hillel House. The late-sixteenth-century English medieval design is characterized by irregular massing with a variety of gables with CROCKET finials, heavy stonework with prominent mortar joints, and Gothic detailing. The entrance facade and pavilion, crowned by a crenellated, fortress-like parapet, are based upon Athelhampton Hall in Dorset. Mrs. Lindsay's ancestral swan's crest surmounts the entrance arch. Hood moldings and triple windows look out from above the arched doorway. On the left rises a massive chimney. Narrow, arched windows with leaded panes group in various

233 Bay State Road.

combinations, enclosed by a flat, TABBED-HOOD molding. Their placement on the facade is, however, symmetrical, allowing interior Classical decoration and proportions. The great living-hall windows rise two stories and feature elaborate Gothic carved-trefoil openings.

This living hall provides a dramatic counterbalance to the richly decorated rooms leading off on both sides. From the ceiling hangs a great lantern composed of rich stained-glass panels framed by bronze standing figures and bracketed trefoil arches. A massive hooded fireplace reinforces the Gothic mood. Stone carving was done in place by Hugh Cairns, sculptor of Richardson's Trinity Church porch.

Lindsay imported English craftsmen to carve the dark oak linenfold paneling which sheathes the lower half of the smooth limestone walls. These artisans also created the lavish Georgian Revival mantelpieces and columns and the Jacobean open strapwork balustrade of the great split-run staircase and second-floor balcony. Such dramatic stairhalls were popular in the earlier Colonial Revival–style mansions in nearby Cottage Farm (B6) and elsewhere (D8, 15).

The interior design progresses by stages to embrace fully the Colonial Revival style. The cloakroom to the right of the entrance recreates a small, vaulted chancel or, perhaps, a scholarly monk's cell. This inner sanctum leads through heavy portière drapes down a few broad steps into the library. Here, the dark, oak-paneled riverview room features a plaster frieze and ceiling which incorporate British iconography: the Tudor Rose, Scottish

*225 Bay State Road.*

thistle, pomegranate, and Mrs. Lindsay's swans.

The Georgian Revival–style dining room on the west river side is richly paneled in dark mahogany with garlands of fruits and flowers carved in wood and cast plaster. Ornately swagged Ionic columns line the foyer separating the dark mahogany dining and all-white drawing rooms. Here is the contemporary turn-of-the-century Colonial Revival style in full flower with lavish overmantel classical pilasters and columns and patterned ceiling.

This theatrical setting provided the background for the romantic tastes of its owner and a stage for the lavish entertainment which wealth and position demanded in the golden years before World War I.

*The Living Hall, 225 Bay State Road.*

## D5a/Trachtenberg Park

Site of Wilson mansion, J. P. Rinn, 1902; later residence of Cardinal, Boston Archdiocese; burned/demolished.

At the corner of Granby Street, two landscaped parks form an entrance to Bay State Road. The waterside park is the site of the now-destroyed Wilson mansion, built in the Colonial Revival style of tan Roman brick and crowned by a white roof balustrade.

In 1970, a fire destroyed this corner mansion. The ravaged site was reclaimed and landscaped into a park through the generosity of Stephen J. Trachtenberg.

## D5b/211 Bay State Road

Rowhouse, Arthur Vinal, 1899; Newman House. Private.

In 1912, Wilson sold his corner mansion to the Catholic archdiocese,

which also purchased the adjoining rowhouse at #211. After the construction of the chancery and cardinal's residence in Brighton in 1926, Notre Dame Academy occupied these premises. The Newman Club for Catholic students now occupies the westernmost rowhouse in a "speculator block" at #211–201 (D7).

*Transoms, 214–206 Bay State Road.*

## D6/214–208 Bay State Road

Rowhouses, Arthur Vinal, 1899; University dormitories.

Lavish corner mansions were not the only building type on Bay State Road.

Alongside these custom designs, builders and architects teamed up to produce row housing. These grouped, single-family units were economical imitations of high-style forms. The long sweep of the large-scale composi-

tions provides a dramatic and coherent streetscape.

Here at #214–208 and at #211–201 (D7), Boston City Architect Arthur Vinal (1884–85), collaborated with his brother, Warren, a local builder. The spatial organization and ornamentation of the tan, Roman-brick-and-limestone-trimmed facades show the sure hand of an expert in the Colonial Revival style (B31). Framing the block are full-height four-story end-bays faced in limestone and crowned by a metal dentil-and-modillion cornice. The intermediate bays rise only three-and-one-half stories and feature a lighter cornice with smaller recessed windows on the top story (A7).

Under a tight budget, ornament was concentrated on window and door enframements. Window treatment graduates from bracketed limestone sills and carved lintels at the first-floor parlor level to the second-level unadorned moldings, broken keystone lintels, and a single curved bracket. On the top floors, detail lessens; the smaller windows suggest the less-formal family and servant uses within.

Vinal, a well-trained architect, individualized each entrance, drawing on rich Classical Revival vocabulary. At #214, free-standing Ionic columns support a balustraded portico; at #212, a deeply carved half-round hood rests upon lavish ENGAGED Corinthian COLUMNS; and at #210, simple Doric columns support a triangular pediment and frame a half-round transom.

Machine-made adaptations provided economically luxurious Colonial details available in the eighteenth century only to the rich. Oak wainscoting and a fireplace usually dominated the large center living-hall. Two- to three-stage staircases with

finely turned spindles and molded railings further enriched these spaces.

These long, narrow dwellings posed problems in lighting and ventilation. Sunlight entered a central reception hall through a stained-glass skylight above the stairwell and from the outside rooms flanking the hall through double POCKET DOORS. Bay windows and high ceilings further increased the sense of space. These interior floor plans adapted well to dormitories when the buildings were converted to university use in 1962.

## D7/211–201 Bay State Road

Rowhouses, Arthur Vinal, 1899; dormitories.

To distinguish these units from those at #214–208, the Vinal brothers varied the materials and distribution of decorative elements. Historic Beacon Hill bowfronts inspired a Federal-style six-unit project. To create a mansion-like illusion, Vinal integrated the units horizontally by sheathing the first-floor base in limestone and stretching across the roofline a classical parapet of alternating open BALUSTERS and closed panels. Then, to break up the resulting large mass, he repeated the formula at #214–208 by raising the end bays the full four-and-a-half-story height while reducing the middle bay projections to three-and-a-half stories; and to introduce variety on an otherwise sober facade, he alternated polygonal with half-round bay shapes and varied the Colonial Revival window sash. Only on the first floor is there a note of luxury: an impressive set of limestone pilasters supports a classical pediment.

*211–201 Bay State Road.*

## D8/191 Bay State Road

Means mansion/townhouse, Little and Browne, 1897; 1940, Harriet Richards House, first cooperative dormitory in the United States.

This is one of the earlier homes on Bay State Road, built before any stylistic patterns were established for the street. The building's distinctive brick work (the quoined-stone effect is achieved by recessing every sixth brick string course), and its symmetrical three-bay double window exterior give it an air of stolid dignity. The heavy Georgian balustrade above the ground floor doorway, and the belt course of GREEK RUNNING KEY pattern, provide a clue to the classical motifs employed within; the magnificent French style grille and wrought-iron arched gateway herald one of the unique and striking interior spaces in the City of Boston.

Inside, a small entry hall lined with green marble and brass-studded leather doors envelops the visitor. One mounts a half-flight of stairs, turns, and suddenly emerges into a great two-story Roman atrium. The room is suffused with light, and presents to the startled eye the illusion of an open courtyard. Garden trellises—hand-painted on the FRESCOed walls—rise from the green marble dado to surround a large fountain, now removed. The Greek key pattern of the exterior facade reappears in the border of the mosaic floor, along the stair BANISTER, and under the SOFFIT of the great balcony. The Classical-style balustrade encircling the atrium echoes the exterior balcony.

Light fills the central atrium through interior windows looking out from the adjacent sitting room. This exquisite room is a textbook example of the delicate French eighteenth-century-style favored at the time by such influential tastemakers as Edith Wharton and Ogden Codman. (Cod-

*191 Bay State Road.*

*The Atrium, 191 Bay State Road.*

man noted that the style was able to "create in a busy city an atmosphere of contemplation.") The room still retains its original gold and white decor, along with many original furnishings.

The second-floor vestibule, lined with fluted columns, leads into the paneled library, now converted to student living space. Here, a bay window, whose upper leaded sash frames a stained-glass coat of arms, offers a splendid view of the Charles River.

## D9/179–171 Bay State Road

Rowhouses, E. M. Machado, 1900; University dormitories.

George Wheatland's career illustrates the magnitude of the turn-of-the-century building boom in Boston's streetcar suburbs. Wheatland acquired large landholdings along Bay State Road (D10). Then, as fast as this part of the marshy bay south of the railroad could be drained and filled, he bought up the north side of Mountfort Street (Tour B). When the street railway extended westward along Beacon Street, he acquired frontage there as well. The successful development of his large holdings clearly necessitated a certain formula of construction, which can be studied in the buildings at #179–171.

In contrast to Arthur Vinal (D6, D7), architect Machado mixes his styles indiscriminately in these rowhouses in

*179–171 Bay State Road.*

order to appeal to a broad range of taste. The rusticated brownstone base reflects a popular motif used a generation earlier by H. H. Richardson. On the first floor, brown terra-cotta clay windows and belt courses are cast in flat relief patterns of anthemion, rosette, and swirling foliage in the style of the Italian Renaissance. The doors, however, in a typical speculator potpourri, adopt the Federal Revival style of half-round transoms fitted with delicate leaded-glass patterns.

On the upper stories, Machado continues the Colonial Revival motif by employing terra-cotta bricks with a center keystone to form lintels over the windows. Crowning the third-floor walls and bays, a wide entablature repeats the first-floor Renaissance motifs. Above this, the Colonial Revival recurs in the projecting den-

til/modillion cornice of pressed metal which visually terminates the composition. In order to gain additional floor space yet minimize the height, the architect employs a technique used successfully in the Italianate-style double mansion at 72 Mt. Vernon Street on Beacon Hill (A7) and at 214–208 Bay State Road (D6): he inserts a row of smaller, inconspicuous windows surmounted by a plain entablature and simple pressed-metal cornice. Only the posts of the rooftop balustrade remain.

The interior ornamentation follows the standard Colonial Revival builder's formula. Varnished oak surrounds the red, black, and white marble FIRE-PLACE FACINGS. Rising up the staircases from the machine-carved newel posts, spiral balusters alternate with plain and inexpensive spindles. Partial wainscoting and heavy ceiling moldings further embellish the dining rooms.

*169–159 Bay State Road.*

### D10/167–169 Bay State Road

Rowhouses, Samuel D. Kelley, 1899; University dormitories.

In the hands of a different architect, Samuel D. Kelley (C14), Wheatland's rowhouses are here more restrained in design; they attempt to harmonize with the expensive mansions on the nearby corners.

The four-and-a-half-story red-brick-and-limestone bowfront houses are identical in design and uniform in height; only the end pairs and the center bay windows are grouped, through the use of iron balconies. Smooth quoined limestone sheathes the first story where recessed doors all feature rectangular transoms. Door enframement alternates flat shelf lintels with broken segmental pediments support-ing urns; all are supported on identical brackets. The SPLAYED lintels on the windows of the upper three stories are similarly economical.

At the roofline, a well-proportioned, plain, pressed-metal entablature under a beaded molding and cornice echoes the slightly projecting limestone belt course above the first floor. A single bracketed PLINTH supporting a ball/urn form marks the PARTY-WALLS sep-arating the houses. The interiors are similar to those at #179–171 (D9). The overall cost to Wheatland was probably no more than at D9, built a year later, but the effect is one of fine proportions and quiet restraint, more appropriate to the neighborhood.

The interior ornamentation is stan-dard for such middle-priced units. Sheathing the marble-tiled entry is six-foot high, three-panel white wain-scoting. The CLOSED STRING COURSE at the end of the staircase RISERS pro-

*168 Bay State Road.*

vides a costly detail, but one balanced by simple, inexpensive balusters. Again, on the dining room fireplace, the wood surround is generous, but the brick facing and other modest fireplaces are minimal in cost. Dentil moldings embellish only the principal hall doorways.

## D11/168 Bay State Road

Townhouse, Arthur Vinal, 1901; University dormitory.

This fanciful, European-influenced, private townhouse is an anomaly within the restrained Classical streetscape. Although designed by one of the major architects in the west Back Bay, it ignores the dominant local fashion and reflects his personal sophisticated taste. Arthur Vinal, City Architect (1884–85), trained in the office of Peabody and Stearns. His active career covered a broad range of building types from speculator row housing (often in collaboration with his brother, Warren) to public buildings. This townhouse, with his wife as owner, was probably built on speculation, since the Vinals resided in a fashionable section of Dorchester.

The facade beautifully illustrates the influence upon American designers of the high-style FRENCH CLASSICAL Beaux Arts School. A strong, rusticated, three-bay first level supports two overscaled, richly decorated windows at the second or *premier étage* floor. Half-round window-surrounds of quoined blocks frame the carved concave facings which articulate outward from a flattened segmental arch.

Stone belt courses set apart the top floor and frame the two central levels. Limestone integrates the three-bay first-floor arcade with the quoin trim

of the third-floor windows. The window keystones further act to support the upper belt course and dentil cornice of pressed metal below the parapet.

While Bay State Road gains its significance from the repetition of Classical forms, it is refreshing to find a graceful and individualistic expression along the way.

## D12/157 Bay State Road

Rowhouse, Putnam and Cox, 1903; University dormitory.

In contrast to the series of large speculator units (D6, 7, 9, 10), #157 appears lighter in form and more individual in execution. In deference to the neighboring three-and-a-half-story corner mansions, the architects halted the bowfronts at the third story. To minimize the height, they then recessed the fourth story into a mansard roof with dormers, further screened by the bowfront parapet. Window treatment remained simple; with six-over-six sash in authentic Federal Revival mode, diminishing in scale with each higher floor. However, the brick laid in Flemish bond adds a rich texture to the composition.

## D13/153 Bay State Road

Pitman Mansion, Wheelwright and Haven, 1893; University dormitory.

Corner houses on the cross streets along Bay State Road are generally of a grander scale and form impressive frames for the smaller townhouses between. The main, architecturally dramatic entrances typically face the side street, while the shorter Bay State Road facades are subdued and scaled down to match the Federal-Revival Beacon Hill–like streetscape. While this combination of restraint and imposing grandiosity results in hybrid, individualized compositions, the total vista of Bay State Road remains coherent and impressive.

The mansion at 153, typical of most corner residences on the street, utilized sophisticated visual tricks and expensive designs. Architect Wheelwright (D28) was well known for his English Free Style and Colonial Revival designs, in which he combined authentic elements in an individualistic manner.

The exterior is deceptively simple. Wheelwright visually eliminates the fourth story by recessing the dormers on the HIPPED ROOF. He relieves the great mass of the nearly symmetrical facade by placing the doorway and principal window in the second bay and by projecting slightly the remaining three-bay portion of the mansion. A tall chimney in the fourth bay balances the group.

Ornamentation is limited to the roof parapet with its alternating balustrade and panels and to the delicate filigree balconies which ornament the bow front and Palladian window. The ground-level front door illustrates typical Colonial Revival motifs. Set in an extremely broad half-round arch of limestone, the oversized leaded-glass transom rests upon a three-part wooden pilaster and lintel group. Directly above is a correct Palladian three-part window with half-round center transom within a segmental arch.

Inside the restrained facade, Wheelwright is witty and inventive. Architectural fragments cram the small foyer. Opposite the doorway, a small oriel window with unusual leaded patterns overlooks the entry. The half-flight of stairs curves alongside a recessed wall niche with shell hood to the oversized nine-panel interior door. Opposite the entrance, at the end of the hall, a short run of stairs with three different Georgian-style balusters on each tread turns, then disappears within the wall. Fireplaces vary in treatment: Federal in the hall, Georgian on the paneled library wall. Fitted doors line the dressing rooms. Thus, interior luxury contrasts with exterior restraint.

*153 Bay State Road.*

## D14/152 Bay State Road

Storey mansion, Fehmer and Page, 1902;
University academic departments.

The English architect Richard Norman Shaw, whose designs were widely
published in America, directly influenced Boston architecture in this corner mansion. Fehmer modeled the
house closely on Shaw's London mansion at 170 Queensgate, built in 1887–
88. The four-and-a-half-story building
at #152 features an austere red-brick-
and-brownstone facade crowned by a
roof balustrade with a Palladian dormer incorporating paired chimneys.
Ornament is concentrated on quoins,
curved window APRONS, and a classical door enframement. While changing Shaw's English materials of brick,
concrete, and terra-cotta to Back Bay
brick and brownstone, Fehmer retained the overall massing, the shaped
central roof gable, the window groupings, and the elegant broken pediment
over the entrance door. He enlarged
upon his British model by inserting an
additional floor, and by rounding the
bays at the short ends of the house.

*152 Bay State Road.*

*152 Bay State Road.*

The second or main floor contains two large oval rooms with lavishly plastered ceilings flanking a large central hall through which a great mahogany staircase rises four levels. Fehmer paid homage to Shaw by copying the half-flight of hall stairs containing, at the landing, a recessed seat and by imitating the mantel and right-angled consoles on the marble dining-room fireplace. In particular, he duplicated the fanlight over the front door of the London mansion in the glass cupboards of the Storey dining room. This motif was widely copied in the high-style houses along the street and can be seen in Fehmer's #67 (D27) of 1897 and #141 (D17) of 1900, in Arthur Little's 2 Raleigh Street (D29) of 1890, and in Peters and Rice's elegant design of 1901 at 73 Bay State Road (D25). By adapting these high-style English models, Boston architects proved

themselves able to meet the expectations of Boston's affluent society.

### D15/147 Bay State Road

Weld mansion, Peters and Rice, 1900; Dunn House, University president's offices.

Number 147 stands in splendor above all other campus buildings. In 1900, Dr. William Weld, a prominent sur-

*Transom, by Norman Shaw, 170 Queensgate, London. (Photo by Nancy Salzman)*

geon, commissioned W. Y. Peters to create for him a palatial setting. Leaving the project in the hands of Peters, who had also designed their Brookline mansion and summer house in Maine, the Welds set sail for Europe, where they viewed the Paris Exposition and ordered accessories for their new home. While in Italy, Dr. Weld, whose hobby was woodworking, hired artisans to complete the interiors. W. Y. Peters had purchased lots at 143–5–7 Bay State Road. He retained #143–145 for himself and his brother, Gorham, but gave two feet to the corner man-

sion site. Just how successful the integrated three-unit facade is can be seen by comparing the rear facade with its distinct treatment of each vertical residence. Peters did not employ Weld's builder, G. W. Morrison, to construct his half of the building (D16), though the interior finish of the Peters' townhouses suggests that Weld's Italian carvers found extra employment next door.

The four-story corner block bears strong resemblance to Bryanston, the neo-Baroque country house by English architect Richard Norman Shaw, whose designs were strongly reflected along this street. Heavy limestone ele-

*147–141 Bay State Road.*

*First-floor landing, 147 Bay State Road.*

ments outline the red-brick mansion, integrating the horizontal and vertical features. On the main facade, projecting end pavilions are ornamented by limestone quoins and capped by elaborately carved pediments.

The entrance bay features double rustic columns supporting a large stone balcony onto which open French doors flanked by narrow Shaw-style windows. The segmental broken pediment with CARTOUCHE over these doors adds a Palladian touch. Directly above, carved garlands embellish the round window. Horizontally, a rusticated ground-floor and roof balustrade frame this lavish composition. On the Bay State Road elevation, only tall windows with splayed keystone lintels and projecting balconies hint of the luxury within, thus integrating

with the restrained Federal Revival streetscape. Graceful wrought-iron fencing and a waterside balcony complete the exterior decoration.

Handcrafted bronze, woods, and marbles create a dazzling interior. The ground-floor reception room is open to the second level through an oval balcony. Through this opening can be seen the hand-carved, urn-shaped spindles of the balustrade and, above, the great German chandelier with its three thousand crystal droplets. A double bronze stair balustrade curves on either side around a fountain enclosed within a golden marble shell. Luxurious details abound throughout: French bronze door plates and handles, carved wooden and marble fireplaces, floors inlaid in a variety of woods in remarkable foliage patterns. On the third floor, the quality of design continues. Here is the famous

*145 Bay State Road.*

treasure room where a concealed door guarded the Weld Oriental Collection, now exhibited at the Boston Museum of Fine Arts.

These treasures narrowly escaped destruction. In 1937, George Dodge, manufacturer of embalming chemicals, purchased the building intending to remodel it as quarters for his projected Institute of Anatomy, Sanitary Science and Embalming. In December 1941 Boston University bought out Mr. Dodge and converted the mansion into the College of Practical Arts and Letters (now the College of Basic Studies). As the stateliest building on the campus, it served in the fifties as a faculty club, and now houses the president's offices and meeting rooms for trustees.

### D16/145–143 Bay State Road

Peters brothers townhouses, Peters and Rice, 1900; Weld House, University administration.

These twin townhouses, home of the architect and his brother, continue the high degree of detail on the contiguous Dunn House (D15). The building permits, however, list a different builder, F. L. Whitcomb. On the exterior, evenly spaced windows decrease in height on each floor in a restrained Bulfinch manner. The brothers' entrances share a double portico centered on their combined six-bay block. Unfortunately, the architect's own home, #143, burned and was later converted to Lahey Clinic uses, and the interior was lost. It now contains modern university offices.

A small, first-floor entry to #145 leads through a doorway framed by sidelights in Shaw's fan-tracery. Up a half-flight, the open stairhall features an extraordinary Federal Revival fireplace of green marble, garnished with carved onyx. The staircase carries Georgian style balusters, three different turnings to the tread. Walnut paneling with a dentil cornice sheathes the riverside room on the second floor. Fluted Corinthian pilasters flank a remarkable green-marble fireplace-and-overmantel composition—the finest carving to be found on the entire campus. Inspired by the extraordinary seventeenth-century English carver, Grinling Gibbons, it depicts realistic fruits, flowers, leaves, ribbons, and shell-and-cartouche coats-of-arms. How fortunate that only two owners preceded the university as stewards of this treasure and how tragic that the architect's own home next door passed through a succession of uncaring owners.

## D17/141 Bay State Road

Townhouse, Fehmer and Page, 1900; University administration.

The firm of Fehmer and Page (D14) was renowned for its use of high-style motifs, unusual brickwork, and complex spatial relationships. Fehmer emigrated from Germany and by 1861 had arrived in Boston. After a collaboration with William Emerson, the lively exponent of the Queen Anne style from 1867 to 1875, Fehmer (and later Page), embarked on a successful high-style practice in commercial as well as domestic buildings. Shortly after the completion of #152 in 1902,

the sixty-five-year-old Fehmer left Boston, probably in retirement.

In contrast to the taut, planar facades along Bay State Road, here at #141, a three-sided bay overhangs the ground-floor entrance and rests upon square, fluted piers connected by a low brick wall. This provides a sense of depth and forms an architectural counterpart to the monumentally scaled ten-bay composition by William Y. Peters at numbers 143, 145, and 147 next door.

Decoration is minimal. Limestone lintel and belt courses group together the three middle floors, whose windows decrease proportionally in size. The plain brick parapet, capped in stone, supports urns which punctuate the skyline and mark the angles of the bay front.

The influence of the English architect R. Norman Shaw again dominates the interior design. Fehmer and Page had experimented with the fan motif in 170 Queensgate, London, at #67 (D27) and would repeat it two years later at 152 Bay State Road (D14). At #73 (D25), #145 (D16), and 1 Raleigh Street (D30) the fan also appears. A full-length triple window whose mullions form this characteristic open-fan fills the walls of the ground-floor entry and repeats in the cupboards of the first-floor riverview dining room. Shaw frequently incorporated benches in halls and on stair landings. Here, Fehmer includes a corner bench whose armrest is formed by an exaggerated S-curve post and pierced SPLATS reminiscent of the open-fan motif.

Thus #141 typifies the intelligent awareness of European aesthetic trends among the high-style Boston architects at the turn of the century and serves to illustrate the balance be-

*125–121 Bay State Road.*

tween the socially acceptable Federal Revival streetscape and the current fashionable design trends behind the sober doors.

## D18a/125 Bay State Road

Sophie Moen double mansion, Winslow, Wetherall and Bigelow, 1899; University offices.

In startling contrast to its neighbors is this Italian Renaissance–derived palazzo. The Moen sisters' desire for pretentious residences probably led their architects to model their work after the sensational 1883 Villard Mansion in New York City by McKim, Mead and White (now part of the Helmsley Palace Hotel). According to Henry Forbes Bigelow "the architect proba-

bly contributed more to the creation of charming and distinguished house interiors than any other person of his time." Although a few examples of this style appear in the Back Bay (412, 420 Beacon Street), this palazzo is certainly not in keeping with the conservative Bostonian desire to continue Federal and Greek Revival Beacon Hill models. Upon closer examination, however, this domineering, U-shaped, stone double townhouse does, in fact, adapt to the Bay State Road scale.

The broad exterior stairs and terrace lead to the striking loggia of four green-marble columns supporting a balustrade which defines the entrance porch and connects the two projecting side pavilions. Horizontal divisions and sharply framed windows characterize the smooth ASHLAR limestone facade. BELT COURSES divide the two

143

principal floors from the basement and attic rooms, whose smaller-scaled windows announce their lesser, domestic functions. A closed balustrade with swagged panels forms a parapet and crowns the entire symmetrical design.

Within #125, a side entry leads into a dramatic hall space enriched by a marble pavement and panels formed by moldings. An oval staircase with ornate bronze railing curves gracefully toward the Adam-style skylight above. To the right of the stairhall, in the former dining room, dark paneling with embossed leather-like wallcovering frames the river view. Above, a great molded plaster garland encircles the spectacular white coved ceiling. In the parlor facing Bay State Road, the restrained, vertical floor-length windows echo the narrow rectangular green-marble fireplace in French Classical style, with its plaster-swagged overmantel mirror (B6, D30).

The formal balance of the principal rooms changes abruptly in the third floor where fireplaces, cabinets, and closets are deliberately off center, thus revealing a turn-of-the-century interest in eclectic combinations of styles.

rored windows set into the walls, another Richard Norman Shaw motif used extensively along Bay State Road. The ornate balustrade displays an open bronze grille in which the entwined initials "A" and "C" alternate with *fleur-de-lys* set within a lyre. Open S and C curves enframe both motifs.

Nineteenth-century architectural theory classified styles and uses as masculine or feminine. For example, the delicate Classical parlor was considered feminine. Here, subtle paneling with applied ROCOCO motifs and a cove ceiling with narrow egg-and-dart molding create a chaste, quiet FRENCH CLASSICAL feeling, so strongly recommended by Codman. A low, gray-marble fireplace with wide consoles supporting a tall Regency-style mirror adds dignity to the riverfront room. On the other hand, Gothic, Jacobean, or rustic motifs were considered virile and adventurous. The dark oak-paneled dining room facing the street is dominated by a hand-carved Jacobean-style fireplace with stone surrounds and a patterned iron firebox. Gothic moldings and leaded bay window embellish the third floor "for men only" billiard/smoking room.

## D18b/121 Bay State Road

Alice Moen Childs double mansion, Winslow, Wetherell and Bigelow, 1899; University admissions visitors center.

Number 121 is more elaborate than its twin. A circular marble hall relates the curving bronze staircase and the three rooms that lead off at both ends. The staircase curves past oval mir-

## D19/128 Bay State Road

Hurd, Gore, 1913; University Naval Science Department.

At first glance, this fine rowhouse block of #128 respects the typical streetscape. Here, lesser-known Boston architects composed a conservative, three-and-a-half-story red-brick-and-limestone building with the appropriate Federal Revival doorway and ironwork. In fact, this house was not

*Interior, 125 Bay State Road.*

built until 1913, but it maintains a model common to the street since the turn of the century. Three years earlier, next door at #110–118 (D20), a whole new idiom had already come into use.

The interior continues in an extremely conservative (and financially safe) manner. It maintains the center hall plan, reproduces the speculator-style mosaic-and-wood-paneled entry, and combines Georgian and Federal details in the fireplace ornamentation. The only change in the direction of #110–118 seems to appear in the lower, more modest height of the ceiling and broader, muscular proportions of the windows.

## D20/110–118 Bay State Road

Rowhouses, E. B. Stratton, 1910; rentals, University administration.

These rowhouses form the most eclectic group on the road and illustrate the ways in which a speculator-developer

could individualize his product. Built in different types of brick, and in totally different styles, each unit remains three bays wide and three stories high, a half-story lower than other buildings in the area, most of which had been constructed earlier. Passing through a succession of owners, these speculative houses were divided into small apartments, with the exception of #118, the home of Dr. Frank Lahey, late director of the nearby Lahey Clinic (C8).

The interior designs are similar and the floor plans identical. On the first floor, the double entrance-doors lead directly into a living room with the side staircase of well-turned spindles along one wall, the fireplace opposite. Ahead, another double door leads between columns to the rear dining room and pantry. Simple beams articulate the relatively low ceilings of both rooms. Classical Revival–style fireplaces throughout feature decorative iron firebacks.

On the exterior, #118 combines the two upper floors into one unit. Vertically, side pilasters composed of yellow-brick panels framed by flat,

*110–118 Bay State Road, circa 1910. Center building is now vacant lot. (The Brickbuilder, 1910)*

rusticated quoins flank triple-sash windows set in metal frames and spandrels. Horizontally, a rusticated first floor and a metal roofline frieze, modillion, and balustrade balance the window composition.

Number 116 repeats its neighbor #118 with the rusticated stone first floor, the center portico and the frieze, modillion cornice, and vertical stone framing of the middle floors. Here, however, the wall surface is red brick with prominent mortar joints. Full-length windows with pretentious stone surrounds and bracketed heads fill the second level. On the third floor, three stone panels below three smaller windows adhere to the second-floor scale. The impression is of a house twice its actual size. Number 114 was demolished for a second, out-of-scale, modernistic structure no longer on the site.

Number 112 is the most imaginative in the row. The first floor follows standard classical rules with a richly carved segmental hood over the double doors. On the middle floors, the window composition of sash, casement, and spandrel framed by giant pilasters repeats that of #118. But suddenly, the architect, Stratton, bursts into Mediterranean or Mission style (C28). The pilasters of yellow brick feature a tapestry design of diamond and cross in contrasting brick, while a sloping red-tile roof with exposed rafters rises over the flat, white, modillion cornice.

Number 110 presents an almost overpowering use of Federal Revival vocabulary within a modest residential scale. The designer closely copied the imposing Portsmouth, New Hampshire, Athenaeum (1803–05) by Bradbury Johnson, itself influenced by Charles Bulfinch's Massachusetts

State House. Around the single doorway, the architect, Stratton, extends the sidelights up and over the fanlight, forming a second arch. This motif, used earlier in Arthur Little's mansion at 2 Raleigh Street (D29), would be repeated again by Arthur Bowditch in the 1935 Myles Standish Hotel (D31). The two upper stories are integrated within a typical Bulfinch composition of two-story, white pilasters supporting a white frieze with modillion cornice. Grouped within these vertical elements are slender six-over-six sash windows with keystone lintels.

The first client for this single-family speculator-built home was a middle-class dry-goods merchant. As the neighborhood changed uses, #110 served as a School of Speech Therapy and then as an apartment house. It is now rental housing.

## D21/55 Deerfield Street

Brooks Mansion, Shepley, Rutan and Coolidge, 1900; rental.

Number 55 is unusual in its near-trapezoidal plan, designed to fit an irregular lot. The architectural firm (in which Shepley was a successor to H. H. Richardson) created a symbiotic relationship with its large neighbor to the east by combining commissions for the two separate owners on this site (cf. D15, 16, 18a and b). Although it occupies only one ground floor bay along Bay State Road, the Brooks house appears to encompass the whole facade of 99 Bay State Road.

The tautness of detailing and the understated use of carefully balanced Classical motifs and proportions give the building a slightly austere grandeur. Wrought-iron scroll work and

*55 Deerfield Street.*

vertical grillage cover the ground-floor windows and glass entrance doors. Woven into the front-door grille are the initials of its first owner, Peter Brooks, who himself had a major impact upon American architecture. With his brother, he invested in Chicago real estate, admonishing his agent that the building's use should determine its aesthetics. The resulting Monadnock, Marquette and Rookery Buildings inaugurated the "Chicago style" of commercial architecture.

The entrance consists of prominent stone Doric columns IN ANTIS which support a triglyph-and-metope entablature, dentil cornice, and swelling balcony above. The windows of the "piano nobile" level gain height through the use of panels inset above the six-over-six pane sash. Splayed limestone separated by brick forms the lintels here and on the third story. The roof parapet is composed of limestone piers and railings which alternate solid brick panels with open grillework above the windows. Originally, a three-bay room led onto the rooftop terrace. This terrace has been filled in with a clumsy modern addition which, with the necessary fire escape, spoils the original concept.

### D22/91 Bay State Road

Sheraton Apartment Hotel, Strickland, Blodgett and Law, 1923; Shelton Hall (University dormitory).

In the mid-1920s, luxury apartment hotels (D31) advertised "an appealing

For illustrated Brochure
or for a personal inter-
view call on our repre-
sentative at The Shera-
ton or communicate with
W. H. Ballard & Co., Inc.,
45 Milk Street, Boston

TO those who are accus-
tomed to a cultured
home of ample means, The
Sheraton presents an appealing counterpart, which includes the advantages of a
modern apartment hotel.
Exclusive and commanding
in location — close by the
beautiful Charles — but a
minute from Kenmore sta-
tion—convenient to "busi-
ness"-Boston—the Sheraton
represents the highest type of
home-like, non-housekeep-
ing residence hotel. In quality and simplicity of appoint-
ments, it is distinctly characteristic of that distinguished style and period—
—"The Sheraton." Recently
completed—now open for
occupancy. You are invited
to visit and inspect at your
leisure, The Sheraton.

## *The Sheraton*
### *91 Bay State Road*

**W. H. BALLARD & CO., INC., RENTING AGENTS**
45 MILK STREET    TELEPHONE CONGRESS 6202

*Promotional announcement issued on the opening of "The Sheraton" in 1923. (Society for the Preservation of New England Antiquities)*

counterpart to those who are accustomed to a cultured home of ample means." In their prospectus, the owners, who had engaged the designers of the "ultimate" in Boston hotels, the Ritz-Carlton, advertised the Sheraton:

> In quality and simplicity of appointments it is . . . characteristic of that distinguished style and period, the Sheraton. . . . Baths are equipped with the most modern fixtures. . . . Floors are all highly polished oak. . . . Pantries on each floor make prompt and easy service possible in every suite.

When Ernest Henderson and Robert Moore purchased this, their third hotel, in 1939, they discovered the great expense of replacing the rooftop electric sign, and decided instead to retain "Sheraton" as their new corporate logo.

The Sheraton achieved national fame. From its rooftop ballroom, CBS and NBC radio broadcast the well-known weekend dance bands, while formally attired guests were served by white-coated waiters. Eugene O'Neill came here to live in May 1951, and it was in Room 401 on November 27, 1953, that the famous author died.

Sensitive to the streetscape, the architects broke down the massive eight-story brick building into a U-shape with horizontal belt courses and decorated it with the neighborhood's Federal Revival formulas. Detail concentrates upon the limestone two-story entrance whose giant pilasters support a graceful broken pediment. Carving is flat and delicate. Window lintels on the lower stories carry a center panel of carved hexagonal medallions with rosettes which flank a Sheraton-style swagged urn, elongated in shape rather than solid and upright as in the Georgian mode.

Inside, classical moldings enrich the lobby. A Palladian-style doorway opens into the dining room. A Federal-style frieze surmounts each door. The public dining room ceiling carries heavy coffered beams with PENDANTS. Encircling the wall is a frieze of triglyphs and rosettes. A portion of the diamond parquet oak floor still survives here inside a small closet.

## D23/83 Bay State Road

Fox and Co., 1900; later the Joslin Clinic; rental.

Dr. Elliott P. Joslin, a pioneer in the study of diabetes, established his clinic next to his home at #81. There is evidence that this house was the right-hand twin of a building now destroyed, with the original first-floor entries grouped as a pair. Note the first-floor triple window with brick repair below, and the ground-level entrance, probably relocated from the first floor during these alterations.

The end-of-the-century Classical Revival included Greek as well as Federal forms. Here, CLASSICAL GREEK REVIVAL details ornament the townhouse. A Greek fret pattern (D8, 27) embellishes the stone window lintels. The open gable-parapet is also Greek in inspiration; its frieze incorporates an anthemion-leaf motif (D27).

The most dramatic feature is the two-story ironwork balcony, evoking the early nineteenth-century craftsmanship displayed on Beacon Hill, itself inspired by eighteenth-century London terrace houses. The upper balcony of late Greek Revival designs contrasts curiously with the lower balustrade of Federal Revival–style medallion inserts. The graceful curved roof of VERDIGRISED COPPER is typical

*83–81 Bay State Road.*

of the English Regency style of the same date.

## D24/81 Bay State Road

Townhouse, Fox and Co., 1900; later Dr. Elliott P. Joslin home; University dormitory.

The modest restraint of the red-brick Federal Revival exterior gives no hint of the spacious and detailed interior. A half-flight of stairs leads up from a simple entry into an elegant oval stairwell where the richly fluted newel post recalls the historic and much-copied 1746 John Hancock House. The stairs curve upward past a wall niche to the upper hall, which extends the full width of the townhouse. Here the open stair spindles form a balcony and are fitted with a built-in seat. The design vocabulary then shifts from Federal to Greek Revival, where a clerestory row of square windows set with cross-mullions (cf. Morse Auditorium [C9]) funnels light into the hall from the front room. Around this large center hall runs a rich cornice with a paneled soffit studded with little knobs called "guttae."

## D25/73 Bay State Road

Townhouse, Peters and Rice, 1901; rental.

Is this the *most* beautiful house on Bay State Road? Here, architects combined R. Norman Shaw's earlier Queen Anne motifs with the Federal Revival style in a highly original manner. The upper three stories of the four-and-a-half-story, three-bay townhouse are in the Federal Revival mode; red-brick stretchers alternate with blue headers in a Flemish bond pattern.

The first-floor oriel window is mag-

nificent. Based directly on Shaw's New Zealand Chambers, itself derived from the sixteenth-century Sparrowe's House in Ipswich, England, it is a variation on a Palladian window. Graceful quarter-round windows join the wide, projecting center sash to the end panes which lie flush within the wall. Rows of diamond shapes, banded top and bottom by circles, separate a diminutive tracery of vertical leaded mullions. Rich garlands made up of intricate bits of glass overlay a similar composition in the transoms.

The doorway is equally striking. Simple stone Ionic pilasters support a lintel with dentil cornice. Within this is a slender, delicate wooden frame. Attenuated columns with tiny fluting support a lintel of narrow, running fret molding, from which springs a half-round transom arch. The tracery is, once again, Shaw's 170 Queensgate fan (D14, 16, 27, 30) (repeated in the drawing-room transom), complete with house number, although here overlaid with a four-part swag of myrtle leaves. An open urn with swags and scrolls set within a double frame filled with more filigree also embellishes the single pane of door glass. Thus, within a small space, and on even a smaller scale, a wealth of ornament blossoms forth.

On the second level, recessed blind relieving arches within a broad stone frame recall Bulfinch's famous Second Harrison Gray Otis house at Mt. Vernon Street, Beacon Hill. Within the arch, the half-round, louvred fan-transom above the window and the lacy-filigree iron balconies below give the illusion of floor-length windows. The parapet, as next door at #75, alternates closed panels with thin, urn-shaped balusters.

## D26/71–69 Bay State Road

Townhouses, Chapman and Frazer, 1897; rental.

A contemporary magazine praised "the home-like quality for which this firm is always noted and its details which are full of delicacy and refinement." Both houses are identical in scale, mass, and projecting bay element, but they draw upon different architectural sources for detailing.

In #71, the architects for the Castle (D4) employ Tudor elements in the second-floor triple window hood, third-floor arched diamond-paned windows, and carved medieval bosses of the belt cornice. The iron balcony is composed of medieval quatrefoils, trefoil arches, and *fleur-de-lys* finials. The parapet alternates closed panels with open Jacobean strapwork. However, on the second floor, the Shaw-influenced, three-part oriel windows show their Palladian origins clearly and may have prompted the design of #73 next door. The rear elevation is intact—a rare occurrence in this neighborhood.

Number 69 is a mirror image of #71, but in tan brick with Colonial

*73 Bay State Road.*

Revival detail. A prominent portico of Ionic columns supports a dentil cornice from which springs a wooden arch faced with a frieze of alternating triglyphs and medallions. Federal Revival tracery frames the glass casements in the first-floor bay.

On the second floor, windows with fan transoms flank a Palladian triple window within a shallow segmental arch. The heavy modillion cornice above the two middle levels repeats at the roofline. The parapet is similar to its twin at #71 but incorporates classical balusters instead of open Jacobean strapwork.

Inside, a small, leaded bay window overlooks the entry (cf. D13). A long, paneled hall leads to a half flight of stairs, relocated when the house was made over into apartments. Here, a half-round Federal-style window provides a glimpse of the river. The second-floor dining room is thoroughly original and asymmetrical. On the river wall, an inglenook with leaded glass in the upper sash takes advantage of the view. A broad, oversized fireplace wall with mantel shelf supported by columns dominates the long party wall. The opposite wall, paneled three-quarters up, contains opaque, leaded-glass windows over a forceful Classical frieze (D2).

### D27/67 Bay State Road

Townhouse, Fehmer and Page, 1897; rental.

Superb Greek Revival–style metalwork dominates the mixture of Classical styles on this facade. Georgian rustication and splayed window lin-

*71–69 Bay State Road.*

155

tels on the ground floor form a strong base for the Federal Revival two-story Roman brick pilaster and entablature composition above. The high-style architects, Fehmer and Page (D14, 17), announced the dominant Greek Revival style in the strong post-and-lintel doorway and its heavy double doors with deep-carved acroteria and rectangular transom, and in Greek running key motifs with rosettes ornamenting the projecting limestone belt course and lintel end-blocks.

Imposing black cast-iron balconies and porch balustrades add an air of solid craftsmanship and quality to the building. At the roofline, the void between the neighboring four-story townhouses provides an effective foil to the copper roof CRESTING in Greek anthemion-leaf pattern (D23).

While the simple geometric openings pale alongside the luxurious neighbors at #71 and #69, this expensive decorative program hints of an equally lavish interior within. Again, the R. Norman Shaw fanlight motif (D14, 16, 27, 30) appears in the dining-room china-cupboard door.

## D28/61–59 Bay State Road

Double townhouses, Edmund M. Wheelwright for himself, 1893.

Wheelwright's decision to settle in this new district next door to the architect Arthur Little further reinforced the artistic flavor of the neighborhood. While social connections played a large role in the granting of architectural commissions, Wheelwright (and the other designers) could also use their own houses as models to illustrate their taste and standards of craftsmanship. As such, the home

of the City Architect (Wheelwright's term was 1891–95) is an important landmark.

Wheelwright occupied one of a pair of red-brick, Flemish-bond townhouses in strict Federal Revival style, four and a half stories, with a bow front and a more modest fourth story across the top. Ornamentation on the upper floors is spare. A thin stone belt course divides the second from the third floor; stone keystones above the six-pane-over-six-pane upper windows and balconies linking the two houses recall early nineteenth-century Beacon Hill.

*67 Bay State Road.*

All detailing concentrates on the first level. The paired doors with glass sash recess modestly within brick arches only four steps up from the sidewalk. The door lintel resembles a

fireplace surround with its five-part composition and narrow dentil molding. Only the intricate lead tracery in a fan pattern enriches the entrance. A single large, projecting copper lantern links the two doorways.

First-floor windows echo Bulfinch's Third Harrison Gray Otis house at 45

*61–59 Bay State Road.*

*2 Raleigh Street.*

Beacon Street in the six-over-six-over-six sash which opens onto individual iron-filigree balconies. Limestone window enframement consists of a narrow decorated console supporting the frieze and projecting modillion cornice.

The interior plan dramatizes a central stairhall and oval, riverview dining room. Thus the sophisticated Wheelwright combines judicious selection with careful arrangement of Federal forms.

### D29/2 Raleigh Street

Arthur Little mansion, Arthur Little, 1890.

One of the earliest and finest houses in the Bay State Road Historic District, this building stands at the corner of Raleigh Street (so named by the house's owner and architect, Arthur

*The Ballroom, 2 Raleigh Street, circa 1895. (Society for the Preservation of New England Antiquities)*

Little, after the noted Elizabethan personage he often portrayed in the fashionable game of charades).

Educated at M.I.T. and in Europe, Little took a particular interest in Colonial American architecture; and, according to Withey, he came to be considered "a pioneer in reviving and adapting styles in the seventeenth and eighteenth centuries to buildings of his own era." Indeed, 2 Raleigh Street was hailed by the local press as—

> being constructed of material taken from a number of old Colonial houses, some parts being upwards of 200 years old, the whole forming a most unique and artistic combination and a notable evidence of Mr. Little's architectural skill.

The building combines inventive spatial composition and elegant but restrained sophistication within a strict classical precedent. The low, hipped roof and the two-story ballroom have strong allusions to Charles Bulfinch's 1805 Jonathan Mason house, which stood on Mt. Vernon Street, Beacon Hill. Upon closer observation, there appear unexpected shifts among balanced groupings of different floor heights, which read as the reverse-image of the Little-designed companion facade opposite at #1.

The wide Raleigh Street facade integrates three distinct parts vertically. The left ballroom bay is wider. Here, a blind relieving arch continues the Bay State Road facade of two oversized, one-and-a-half-story half-round windows with arching sidelights (D20, 30). In the center section, Little in-

*The Parlor, 2 Raleigh Street, circa 1895.*
*The owner-architect Arthur Little is stand-*
*ing against the wall. (Society for the Preser-*
*vation of New England Antiquities)*

serted an extra floor by lowering the
ceiling heights and placing the oversized double door entrance off center.
The riverview section is as tall and
formal as the ballroom portion.

In the interior, Little abandons the
rectangular rooms and long corridors
of the conventional Victorian house
for an open, flowing, modern treatment of interior spaces. In contrast to
the austere, subtly defined Federal Revival exterior, the interior is rich in
sculptural Georgian Revival decor. In
the living hall and parlor, a half flight

up from the simple entry, ornament is
lavished upon the fireplace walls. Little revels in a dramatic vocabulary of
moldings, scrolls, swags, niches, and
cupboards.

On the second floor, two great
street-side windows light the vaulted
ceilings and chandeliers of the large
double-cube Colonial Revival-style
ballroom. Here a mirrored soffit, set
with bronze ORMOLU, embellishes the
underside of the second floor viewing-
balcony (now closed off). From the
hall, a twisted-baluster staircase leads
to the middle, lower, and more inti-
mate section. The library fireplace,
placed off center, is faced with unusual painted tiles, typical of English

craftsmanship of the period. Such fireplace tiles reappear in different patterns in the bedrooms, frequently in combination with slender Colonial Revival double columns.

Oval-shaped riverview rooms continue the spatial games. In the second-floor dining room, reflecting the French classical influence of Wharton and Codman (B6, D8, 18b, 30), CARYTID pillars support the low fireplace, whose tall overmantel-mirror and drapery cornices have narrow wood frames with ormolu decoration.

Thus Arthur Little, architect and interior designer, indulged his collector's passions and his fantastic imagination. The house, however, was so far out of town that he complained that he was unable to sell it. Ten years after he began his high-style work in the area, his creation was finally bought by a lawyer, who occupied it until 1927. Since 1956, it has served as a dormitory for the university.

## D30/1 Raleigh Street

Leland mansion, Little and Browne, 1893.

Close attention should be paid to this remarkable and complex structure. Its idiosyncratic Raleigh Street facade is a cleverly designed upside-down foil to #2 opposite, while the Bay State Road front presents a different design idiom, one inspired by Charles Bulfinch's Third Harrison Gray Otis House at 45 Beacon Street. This use of the Federal Revival style at #1 and #2 established the pattern for the entire streetscape.

Not content with combining the two different facades, Little garnished them with elaborate ironwork and trim which the *Brickbuilder* stated

"recalls some old London work of the Georgian era . . . the marble and wrought iron details are exquisite." (The later fifth-floor alteration and sixth-floor addition destroy the building's integrity and should be ignored.)

The sedate "Bulfinch" facade on Bay State Road follows the formula of graduated window sizes within a two-story, middle-level pilaster composition. Above a low ground floor, the second-floor six-over-six windows lie within white recessed arches. On the third floor, which serves as the PIANO NOBILE, taller, twelve-over-nine sash windows echo the ballroom of #2. This third-floor dominance continues along Raleigh Street in a great Palladian window. In the center section, the squat proportions of the ground and first floors correspond to those of the top two floors at #2 and successfully act as a platform for the principal third floor. Heavy, low, paired Doric columns supporting a balustrade of urn-shaped turnings enrich the swelling bowfront. Handsome metalwork grilles protect the oversized square windows flanking the entry and echo the elaborate iron fencing and hollow posts.

The interior blends eighteenth-century French and English motifs. From the low-paneled entry ornamented with niches, a half-stair opens through a triple arch into a vaulted high hall. Mirrored French doors lead to the oval river room, ornamented with pilasters; but this room is only a prelude to what must be one of the most magnificent interiors on the tour. The third-floor living hall writhes with raised, curving, swirling rococo panels. A large overmantel mirror encased in this trim almost buries the restrained Classical marble fireplace below. Around the three-stage staircase, a bronze balustrade features the R. Norman Shaw fan, the earliest use of this motif in the houses on Bay State Road. To the right, a few broad steps lead to an oval room, encircled by fluted Corinthian pilasters, where triple, floor-length windows open onto a glorious river view.

How typical of Boston temperament and of Arthur Little's promotion of the understated Federal Revival style that the occupants' wealth lies in private spaces, hidden from the passerby outside.

### D31/30 Bay State Road

Myles Standish Apartment Hotel, Arthur Bowditch, 1925; University dormitory.

*1 Raleigh Street.*

Built in direct competition with the Sheraton apartment hotel (D22), the Myles Standish was described in a prospectus as "one of the finest residential hotels in the country," and its ornately decorated public rooms were the scene of prominent social balls and political gatherings. The architect, Arthur Bowditch, who had been chosen by Boston University to remodel 688 Boylston Street (A11), was responsible for many of the best buildings in the area, and seemed at ease in a variety of styles.

Sited on a vacant, narrowing strip of filled land, the nine-story, E-shaped facade adjusts to the residential character of Bay State Road. Here, the mass divides vertically into three unequal wings. Horizontally, a belt course below the top floor and the limestone sheathing on the first two stories frame the brick block. An arcade featuring large, half-round windows with sidelights connects these blocks at the street level. On commercial Beacon Street, no attempt is made to break up the solid mass, with the exception of vertical, pilaster-like brick quoins. The overpowering scale of this facade illustrates Bowditch's skill in relating to the specific demands of each streetscape.

In the interior, the long, narrow hallway is paneled in dark oak and embellished with fluted pilasters framing bolection-molding panels with doors between. A wide center arch leads to the central vestibule. Hanging on the wall outside the dining room is an oil painting depicting an event in the life of the building's namesake, the Pilgrim father, Myles Standish. Inside the dining room, thin slats of wood, four panels high, inexpensively sheathe the walls. The ceiling is more richly ornamented with heavy beams bordered by dentil and crown moldings. In the hotel's heyday, luxury shops lined the street level.

## D32/632 Beacon Street

Corner Raleigh Street and Bay State Road, Lumberman's Mutual Fire Co., Bellows and Aldrich, 1920; University dormitory annex of D31.

Across Bay State Road is the rear of a symmetrical, three-and-a-half-story commercial limestone building in the Classical Revival style.

**Walk alongside the building to the main entrance facing Kenmore Square.**

This chaste classical building illustrates the type of archeological accuracy favored by architects of the period. In fact, Bellows was an advisor in the construction of Old Williamsburg, Virginia. A half-round arch with Colonial Revival fanlight transom modestly offsets the ground-level entrance. All windows recess within their frames. Balustrades form a belt cornice which projects outward from the flat facade. Centered within each unit projecting Doric columns supporting an entablature and triglyph pediment enframe the ceremonial window. Projecting sills on brackets highlight the third story. At the roofline, a second balustrade repeats the pattern and groups the two upper floors in the classical manner found along Bay State Road. A handsome carved plaque highlights the front parapet.

*632 Beacon Street.*

## D33/660 Beacon Street

Peerless Automobile Showroom, 1910;
1983, Boston University Bookstore and
shopping center, John Carl Warnecke.

Echoes of past elegance returned to
Kenmore Square in 1983 with the renovation of the Peerless Automobile
Building as the Boston University
Bookstore. Back in 1910, the architects evoked the wealth of nearby Bay
State Road by creating a facade, almost as a billboard, in the vocabulary
of the Georgian Revival Weld mansion
(D15). Following classical canons, a
two-story stone base and heavy modillion cornice enframe the four-story pilasters which divide the front into
arch-like window bays. Here 34' ×
5½' banners in university red and

white herald the shops within and act
as a theatrical gateway to Kenmore
Square. Although the original architects alluded to West Back Bay, they
also introduced the new downtown office construction in the metal window
frames with classical detailing.

The garage and showroom of the
"Golden Age" of the auto give way today to New England's largest bookstore. Shops and services fill a seven-
floor, 70,000-square-foot shopping
center. The open commercial construction proves well suited to a
department-store setting where spe-
cialty areas radiate around an open,
central area. Architectural styles and
periods are used to define different departments, and many pay homage to
the styles in the neighborhood.

Atop this collection of interior architectural styles reigns a popular and
newly-rescued example of "commer-

cial archeology." The famous flashing CITGO sign, a great red triangle within a square (replacing the earlier Cities Service sign in green-and-white neon), stands as a blazing landmark and as a memorial to the automobile showrooms which once dominated Kenmore Square.

## D34/Kenmore Square

During the seventeenth and eighteenth centuries, the area now known as Kenmore Square consisted primarily of marshes and the farm that once

*660 Beacon Street.*

belonged to Judge Sewall, of witch-hanging fame. After 1830, railroad tracks and a road, Brighton Avenue (later renamed Commonwealth), were constructed on a strip of filled land which connected Brookline with Boston. Over the years, more marshes and fens were reclaimed and, eventually, the Muddy River itself was channeled into a conduit pipe under Deerfield Street (D21).

Boston's exploding population pushed westward along the roads and newly-laid trolley tracks. By 1902, house permits were filed for this site, linking the residential development of Bay State Road and Brookline. These homes were never constructed and the site lay vacant.

By 1915, Governor's Square (as it was then called) was becoming a major transportation corridor with automobiles, streetcars, and, one block to the south, railroad passenger and freight lines. The resulting noise and pollution made this property unsuitable for residential use, but as a crossroads, the square was a natural site for automobile salesrooms and associated industries. By 1911, early auto companies had appeared: at 660 Beacon, Peerless; at 665 Beacon, Hudson; and at 642 Beacon, Autogar. The Governor's Square subway was constructed c. 1912.

As the movement to suburbia accelerated, houses on Bay State Road were subdivided into apartments. With the building of the Lahey Clinic, staff doctors converted many of these homes into medical offices. Beginning in the 1950s, the influx of Boston University students created a new demand for fast-food stores, discos, and small shops. Today, the streetscape is a fragmented, raucous battle of signs and shop windows. Owners of the four- and five-story commercial buildings hold vacant space and are undecided about the best and most economic uses.

In 1977, Boston University founded the Kenmore Square Businessmen's Association to help bring concerted attention to the planning needs of the Square. In 1983 the university contributed to its improvement with the renovation of a famous auto-showroom building into the largest bookstore in the Northeast (D33). A modernization program by the city has resulted in a red-brick bus and subway station and well-delineated, safe, trolley car corridors. Kenmore Square as a gateway to the university may finally become an integrated visual space in the 80s.

Bibliography

Annotated Index of Architects

Index of Building Types by Original Purpose

Glossary of Architectural Styles

Glossary of Architectural Terms

# Selected
# Bibliography

*American Architects Directory*, R. R. Bowker Co., New York, various editions, including 1970.

Ault, Warren O., *Boston University: The College of Liberal Arts*, Boston University, Boston, 1973.

Blumenson, John, *Identifying American Architecture*, American Association for State and Local History, Nashville, TN, 1977.

Bunting, Bainbridge, *Houses of Boston's Back Bay*, Belknap Press, Cambridge, MA, 1967.

Collier, Eleanor Rust, Histories of Boston University's School of Theology, School of Business Administration, School of Public Communication, Sargent College, School of Law; typescripts, Boston University, Boston, 1958–62.

Columbia University, *Avery Obituary Index of Architects and Artists*, G. K. Hall Co., Boston, 1963.

Drake, Samuel Adams, *Old Landmarks and Historic Personages of Boston*, Little, Brown and Co., Boston; facsimile, Singing Tree Press, Detroit, 1970.

Harrell, Pauline, and Margaret Smith, *Victorian Boston Today*, Victorian Society of America, New England Chapter, Graphics Etc., Inc., Boston, 1975.

Jordy, William H., American Buildings and Their Architects, Vol. III: *Progressive and Academic Ideals at the Turn of the Twentieth Century*, Anchor Press/Doubleday, New York, 1976.

Kay, Jane Holtz, *Lost Boston*, Houghton Mifflin Co., Boston, 1980.

King, Moses, *King's Handbook of the City of Boston*, Cambridge, MA, 1879.

Muthesius, Stefan, *The English Terraced House*, Yale University Press, New Haven, CT, 1982.

Pierson, William H., Jr., American Buildings and Their Architects, Vols. I and II, Anchor Press/Doubleday, New York, 1976.

Shurtleff, Nathaniel B., *Topographical and Historical Description of Boston*, Boston, 1890.

Stanwood, Edward, *Boston Illustrated*, Houghton, Osgood & Co., Boston, 1878.

Tucci, Douglas S., *Built in Boston*, New York Graphic Society, Boston, MA, 1978.

Wharton, Edith, and Ogden Codman, *The Decoration of Houses*, 1903; Norton Library, New York, 1978.

Whiffen, Marcus, *American Architecture Since 1870: A Guide to the Styles*, The M.I.T. Press, Cambridge, MA, 1981.

Whitehill, Walter Muir, *Boston: A Topographical History*, 2nd ed., Belknap Press, Cambridge, MA, 1968.

Withey, Henry F. and Elsie R., *Biographical Dictionary of American Architects (Deceased)*, Hennessy and Ingalls, Inc., Los Angeles, 1970.

Wodehouse, Lawrence, *American Architects*, Vols. 1 and 2, Gale Research Co., Detroit, 1977.

## Other Publications

Alumni Records of Harvard University and Massachusetts Institute of Technology.

*American Architect and Building News.*

*Architectural Record.*

*The Avery Index to Architectural Periodicals,* 2nd ed., G. K. Hall Co., Boston, 1973.

*The World at Boston University,* (weekly newspaper)

*Bostonia* (Boston University alumni magazine).

*The Brickbuilder.*

Brookline Historical Commission, "Nomination to the National Register of Historic Places of Cottage Farm Historic District."

# Annotated Index of Architects

The information in this index is selective. Dates of birth and other pertinent details are included when known.

"Boston is fortunate in having, more than any other city in the U.S. save one, a greater number of men capable of producing domestic work of such originality in point of view and architectural outlook, that it is generally easy to distinguish their houses at a glance from the ruck and commonplace surrounding them."—*Architectural Review*, 1907

ABBOTT. Firm: Shepley, Bulfinch and Abbott. C3.

ALDRICH, WILLIAM T. (1880–1966). M.I.T., Ecole des Beaux-Arts. Apprenticeship: Carrère and Hastings. Firm: Bellows and Aldrich. A watercolorist and bibliophile, and founder of the Museum of Modern Art in New York (with his sister Abby Aldrich Rockefeller). His residential and institutional Beaux-Arts designs, including the Rhode Island School of Design, were prominent and influential. A8, D32.

ANDREWS, ROBERT DAY (1857–1928). M.I.T. Apprenticeship: H. H. Richardson, 1885. Firm: Andrews, Jacques and Rantoul. Public buildings, east and west wings of Massachusetts State House, residences. B8, B21.

BALLOU, MATURIN M. (1820–1895). Architect and editor of the famous *Ballou's Pictorial Weekly*. A6.

BEAL, J. WILLIAMS (1855–1919). M.I.T. Apprenticeship: W. M. Hunt; McKim, Mead and White. Firm: J. Williams Beal Sons. Plymouth County Court House, churches, apartments. A12.

BELLOWS, ROBERT PEABODY (1878–1957). Firm: Bellows and Aldrich. President Boston Society of Architects, advisor to Old Williamsburg, Virginia. A8, D32.

BERRY AND DAVIDSON. B8.

BIGELOW, HENRY FORBES (1867–1929). M.I.T. Firm: Winslow, Wetherell and Bigelow. "Probably contributed more to the creation of charming and distinguished house interiors than any one person of his time" (Withey). Hotels Touraine and Parker House, Jeweler's and Merchant buildings. B5, D18a, D18b.

BILLINGS, HAMMAT (1818–75). Apprenticeship: Asher Benjamin and Amni B. Young. Firm: H. and J. Billings. Illustrator, architect, and designer. Major buildings: Boston Museum, 1846; Massachusetts Charitable Mechanics Assn., 1860; Wellesley College, 1869–75. A5.

BLACKALL, C. H. (1857–1942). University of Illinois, Ecole des Beaux-Arts. First Rotch Travelling Scholarship, 1884. Leading draftsman for Peabody and Stearns. Firm: Blackall, Clapp and Wittemore. Churches, commercial buildings, theatres, residences, Temple Ohabei Shalom, 1928. C9.

BLODGETT, WILLIAM P. (1885–1946). Harvard, M.I.T., Ecole des Beaux-Arts. Firm: Strickland, Blodgett and Law. Hotels and apartments. D22.

BOGNER, WALTER F. Rotch Fellowship, 1925. Firm: Bogner and Billings. Contemporary-style houses, schools, factories. B13.

BOURNE, FRANK. B8.

BOWDITCH, ARTHUR (active 1893–1941, d. 1941). Architect for Boston University. Working in all styles, he was noted for his terra-cotta work. Seventeen remaining buildings downtown: theatres, hotels, office buildings. A11, B14, B32, C25, D31.

BROWNE. Firm: Krokyn and Browne. D3.

BROWNE, HERBERT (1860–1946). Studied in Paris and Florence. Apprenticeship: Jacques and Rantoul. Firm: Little and Browne. One of the leading firms in Boston, with socially prominent clientele. Remodeled the First Harrison Gray Otis House, which had a strong design influence on Colonial Revival–Bay State Road. D8, D29, D30.

BRYANT, GRIDLEY J. F. (1816–1899). Apprenticeship: Alexander Parris, 1837. Pioneered the large architectural office and the standardized plan, which enabled him to reproduce a massive number of structures. These commercial granite structures were so efficient that after the 1872 fire, one hundred eleven of them were rebuilt to the same plan. Public buildings include the Boston City Hospital and Charles Street Jail. Charles A. Cummings apprenticed in this office. P. 28.

BULFINCH, CHARLES, (1763–1844). The first American professional architect who "practically rebuilt Boston" (Withey) in the British Adamsesque style. Educated by a Grand Tour of Europe, he turned professional after the financial failure of his Tontine Crescent project. His Massachusetts State House (1797) and three houses for Harrison Gray Otis set a standard widely emulated in the Federal Revival style along Bay State Road. A1.

BURKAVAGE. Firm: Van Storch and Burkavage. C4.

CARRÈRE, JOHN M. (1858–1911). In partnership with Thomas Hastings. Advocate of Beaux-Arts functional planning. The firm's most notable design was the New York Public Library. Trained William T. Aldrich in the Classical style.

CHANDLER, JOSEPH C. (1864–1945). M.I.T. An authority and author on Colonial architecture, he was identified with restoration of the Paul Revere House, the Old Corner Bookstore, and the House of Seven Gables. B3.

CHAPMAN, WILLIAM (active 1892–1934). Firm: Chapman and Frazer. Residential and public buildings. D4, 26.

CHASE, WILLIAM C. (active 1894–1954). B24.

CODMAN, OGDEN, JR. (1863–1951). M.I.T. Apprenticeship: J. H. Sturgis (uncle). Ogden was the co-author with Edith Wharton of *The Decoration of Houses* (1897), a highly influential work which extolled the "delicacy, harmony and taste" of the eighteenth-century French Classical style. Tours C, D.

COOLIDGE, CHARLES A. (1858–1936). Harvard, M.I.T. Apprenticeship: H. H. Richardson. Carried on firm as Shepley (brother-in-law), Rutan and Coolidge, the oldest firm in continuous existence today. Boston University buildings relate stylistically to the firm's contemporary work at Harvard and, four decades later (as Shepley, Bulfinch and Abbott), New York Hospital. C2, C3, D21.

COX, ALLEN H. (1873–1944). M.I.T., Ecole des Beaux-Arts. Firm: Putnam and Cox. Public and educational buildings include the Unitarian Universalist Assn. on Beacon Hill and the Boston Athletic Club. D12.

CRAM, RALPH ADAMS (1863–1942). Apprenticeship: Rotch and Tilden. Firm: Cram and Ferguson. Influenced by Ruskin and Morris, Cram was in turn a medievalist, philosopher, theologian, humanist, historian, and social theorist. He founded the Boston Society of Arts and Crafts, was the leading American exponent of Gothic style for churches and colleges, and was the author of the first Boston University master plan. C2, C3; pp. 10, 13, 80.

CUMMINGS, CHARLES A. (1833–1905). Rensselaer Polytechnic Institute. Apprenticeship: Gridley Bryant. Firm: Cummings and Sears. His most prominent designs include the Andover Chapel and new Old South Church, Copley Square. P. 5.

DAVIS, ALEXANDER JACKSON, (1803–1892). Firm: Towne and Davis. Widely read architect and artist who, with A. J. Downing, introduced the Picturesque English style. These romantic Gothic Revival suburban house designs were popular in mid-nineteenth-century America. P. 46.

DESKO, A. S. C13.

DEXTER, GEORGE M. (1802–1872). His massive stone structures with Classical proportions appealed to the Lawrence brothers, who gave him free rein in their Cottage Farm development. B15, B17 (possibly B9).

DOWNING, ANDREW JACKSON (1815–1852). American landscape architect whose work espoused the Picturesque style and whose publications stimulated a mid-century "rural-residence" movement in America. See B1 and B9; p. 4.

EMERSON, WILLIAM (1833–1917). Self-taught, charter member of the Boston Society of Architects. Primarily a residential designer, his sensitive siting, picturesque massing, and use of detail in the Shingle, Queen Anne, and Colonial Revival styles were of the highest standard. A4.

FEHMER, CARL (1835–1923?). German, in Boston by 1861. Address in same building as Snell, then Gilman, Bryant and Sturgis. Office of W. R. Emerson, 1867–75. Firm: Fehmer and Page. Charter member Boston Society of Architects, 1870. Sophisticated, high-style designs of private and institutional buildings: M.I.T.'s Walker Building and McLean Hospital, commercial structures: Kennedy's Building and an early skyscraper. Abroad 1904–14. D14, D17, D27.

FERGUSON, FRANK (1861–1926). Firm: Cram and Ferguson. Construction engineer and general manager. Active in the firm's college work. C2, C3.

FOX, BENJAMIN (active 1897–1907). Fellow of American Institute of Architects. B21, D23(?), D24(?)

FRAZER, HORACE S. (1862–1931). Boston Tech, Yale. Apprenticeship: Cabot and Chandler, Peabody and Stearns. Firm: Chapman and Frazer. Designed many fine homes in Boston area. D4, D26.

GOLDBERG, CARNEY, (1907–1981). Many awards, beginning with a Rotch Fellowship in 1931. Firm: Richmond and Goldberg. C6.

GORE, HENRY W. (active 1905–18). Firm: Hurd, Gore. D19.

GOURLEY, RONALD (b. 1919). University of Minnesota, Harvard. AIA Silver Medal, 1943. Firm: Sert, Jackson and Gourley. C17, C19, C20.

HARTWELL, HENRY W. (1853–1919). Apprenticeship: Hammatt Billings. Strongly influenced by H. H. Richardson. In partnership with William C. Richardson (1854–1935). "Skillful handling of Shingle style and careful attention to interior detail." (Wodehouse, vol. 1). See C26.

HAVEN, PARKMAN B. (1858–1943). Firm: Wheelwright and Haven. Notable public buildings: Horticultural Hall and the New England Conservatory of Music. D13, D28.

HOPKINS, JAMES C. (d. 1908) Boston Tech. Firm: Kilham and Hopkins (1902–24). Homes and public buildings, including Radcliffe College dormitories and city halls. B2.

HOWE, LOIS LILLEY (1864–1964). Boston Museum of Fine Arts Museum School, M.I.T. Firm: Howe and Manning. The first woman member and Fellow of the American Institute of Architects, she was an early advocate of urban planning and the need to research architectural details. Her firm specialized in remodeling homes into the Colonial Revival style. B19.

HURD, HENRY W. (active 1905–18). Firm: Hurd, Gore. D19.

JACKSON, HUSON (*b.* 1913). Stanford, University of Chicago, Harvard. Harleston Parker Award for Holyoke Center. Firm: Sert, Jackson and Gourley. C17, C19, C20.

JACOBS, S. W. B30.

JACQUES, HERBERT (1857–1916). M.I.T. Firm: Andrews, Jacques and Rantoul. Specialized in public buildings including the State House wings. B8, B21.

KAHN, ALBERT (1869–1942). Studied in Germany and with George D. Mason, Detroit. The AIA Award hailed him as an internationally famed "exponent of organizational efficiency, a master of concrete and steel." His unique system of team-practice produced designs for factories and showrooms of almost all the American auto firms (over 1000 for Ford alone) and 18 percent of all the buildings in the United States in 1938 which were designed by architects. C22.

KATELLE, WALTER Engineer/architect for the Metropolitan District Commission (circa 1909). Designed boathouses, waterworks, and public recreation structures. C18.

KELLEY, SAMUEL D. (1840–1938). Friend's School: Providence. Apprenticeship: "an old firm in Boston" (obituary). Typical architect/builder of rowhouses and commercial buildings for clients or on speculation. B25, C5, C14, D10.

KILHAM, WALTER H. (1868–1948). M.I.T., Rotch Fellow, 1898. Firm: Kilham and Hopkins. Architect and historical researcher, author of *Boston After Bulfinch*. Wide range of residences, public buildings, and schools, including designs for Radcliffe College. B2.

KROKYN, JACOB F. (1881–1960), Harvard. Apprenticeship: Coolidge and Shattuck. Firm: Krokyn and Browne. Parker Medal for the Motor Mart Garage. Private and public buildings including the Lowell Institute. D3.

LAW, ALEXANDER F. (See Strickland, Blodgett and Law). D22.

LITTLE, ARTHUR (1852–1925). M.I.T. Europe. Apprenticeship: Peabody and Stearns. Firm: Little and Browne. Combined complex spatial tricks with "pioneering interest in reviving and adapting seventeenth- and eighteenth-century styles to buildings of his own era" (Withey). D8, D29, D30; p. 118.

LITTLE, J. L. B8.

MACHADO, E. M. (*c.* 1898–1907). Another architect/builder in the company of Kelley and Vinal, but less competent in design. D9.

MANNING, ELEANOR (1884–1973). M.I.T. (first woman graduate). Firm: Howe and Manning. Specialized in restoration of old homes. Taught housing and urban planning. B19.

MC KIM, MEAD AND WHITE. This firm "established a tradition [of Renaissance and Classical styles] . . . all over the country (in particular, Boston's Back Bay) by the force of compelling example." (Wodehouse). Pp. 7, 35, 47.

MC LAUGHLIN, JAMES (1834–1923). Designed public buildings, schools and homes. C27.

MOWLL, WILLIAM. B12.

NEAL, J. P. (c. 1875). Early speculator/builder of brick rowhouses at 708 Commonwealth Avenue, the westernmost edge of the Back Bay. C15.

NOCKA, PAUL F. (1904–1981), University of Cincinnati, M.I.T. Firm: Marcus and Nocka. Residential and public buildings, including Peter Bent Brigham, Robert Breck Brigham, and Mt. Auburn Hospitals. B10.

NORCROSS BROTHERS: JAMES A. (*b.* 1831) and ORLANDO (*b.* 1839). Their stonework (quarried from their own pits) and woodcarving gave distinctive character to the Ames Building, Trinity Church, and at least half the designs of H. H. Richardson. Their firm was "without question, the most important construction company in the U.S. in the late nineteenth and early twentieth centuries" (James

O'Gorman, quoted in Wodehouse). The firm continued into the twentieth century adapting to the current styles. B28, C24.

OLMSTED, FREDERICK LAW (1822–1903). America's first and most influential professional landscape architect, whose "emerald necklace" provided Boston with an extensive park system while, at the same time, draining marshes to create new land. Pp. 7, 64.

PAGE, SAMUEL F. (see Fehmer and Page)

PARSONS, E. M. (1903–1967). Harvard. Firm: Somes and Parsons. Commercial, concrete structures sensitive to Moderne and Art Deco influence. C7, C8, C12.

PEABODY, ROBERT SWAIN (1845–1917). Firm: Peabody and Stearns. An outstanding architect, Peabody worked in a great variety of styles "scattered over a great extent of the country." (Wodehouse). As one of the leading partnerships in America, the firm constructed a large number of prestigious downtown buildings and suburban mansions. Blackall, Frazer, Little, Vinal, and Wheelwright all trained in the office.

PETERS, WILLIAM YORK (1858–1938). Studied in Europe, Harvard, Atelier Guadet, San Francisco. Apprenticeship: Sturgis and Brigham. Firm: Peters and Rice. Capable of sophisticated and elegant design, Peters retired because of illness in 1904, leaving the practice to Rice. D15, D16, D25; p. 118.

PRESCOTT, HOWARD B. S. (d. 1935). Firm: Prescott and Sidebottom (1895–1918). B6.

PRESTON, WILLIAM G. (1841–1910). Lawrence Scientific School (Harvard). Trained under his father, Jonathan, and at the Ecole des Beaux-Arts. His prolific civic, commercial and residential practice always reflected the latest styles and "artistic" materials. As architect for nineteenth-century Boston University, he chose the Queen Anne Revival style, in red brick with copper, terra-cotta, stone, and glass ornament. A3, A9, A10.

PUTNAM, WILLIAM E., JR. (1873–1947). Harvard, M.I.T., Ecole des Beaux-Arts. Firm: Putnam and Cox. D12.

RAMSEY, GILBERT MILES, (1892–1945). C21.

RAMSAY, HARRY (active 1910–1962). B16.

RANTOUL, AUGUSTUS NEAL (1864–1934). Harvard. Firm: Andrews, Jacques and Rantoul. Designed the Salem Athenaeum, Brookline High School, and several prominent North Shore residences. B8, B21.

RICE, ARTHUR WALLACE (1869–1934?). M.I.T., Paris. Firms: Peters and Rice; Parker, Thomas and Rice. Large, successful practice. D15, D16, D25.

RICHARDSON, HENRY H. (1838–1886). Preeminent Boston architect whose "elemental order," careful craftsmanship, and integral design altered the course of American architecture. Andrews trained in his office, as did Coolidge and Shepley, who with Rutan became the successor firm. Pp. 6, 59, 67, 181.

RICHMOND, ISADORE, (b. 1893). Rotch Fellowship, 1923. Firm: Richmond and Goldberg. C6.

RINN, J. P. D5a.

RUTAN, CHARLES H. (1851–1914). Apprenticeship: office of Gambrill and Richardson, 1868. One of the chief designers for H. H. Richardson. See Coolidge. D21.

SEARLE, EDWIN. Firm: Searle, Von Storch and Steffian (Philadelphia). C31.

SEARS, WILLARD T. (1837–1920). Apprenticeship: J. F. Bryant. Firm: Sears and Cummings. Old South Church: Copley Square, and Gardner Palace (Isabella Stuart Gardner Museum). P. 5.

SERT, JOSÉ LUIS (1902–1983). Barcelona. Apprenticeship: Le Corbusier. Firm: Sert, Jackson and Gourley. Dean, Harvard School of Design. Emphasized teamwork and the role of city planning. The contemporary Boston University campus complements Sert's Peabody Terrace towers and Harvard Holyoke Center upriver. C17, C19, C20; pp. 13, 80.

SHAW, RICHARD NORMAN (1831–1912). "One of the most representative and versatile of British domestic architects" (Macmillan Encyclopedia), whose designs and details were copied on Bay State Road (Tour D). Shaw introduced the picturesque Old English style, then later adopted the Tudor and Queen Anne Revival styles in townhouses of the 1870s. His later, formal classicism suited the taste of Boston Bay State Road patrons and their architects.

SHEPLEY, GEORGE F. (1830–1903). Washington University, M.I.T. Senior member of H. H. Richardson's successor firm. See Coolidge. D21.

SIDEBOTTOM, WILLIAM Firm: Prescott and Sidebottom (1895–1918). B6.

SOMES, JOHN E. (1879–1919). Harvard. Apprenticeship: Bacon and Hill. Firm: Somes and Parsons. Designed a number of auto-related showroom/garages. C7, C12.

STEFFIAN. Firm: Searle, Von Storch and Steffian. C31.

STRATTON, E. B. (1870–1953). Firm: Stratton and Bowditch. Hotels and residences. D20.

STRICKLAND, SIDNEY T. (b. 1880). M.I.T., Ecole des Beaux-Arts. Apprenticeship: C. H. Rutan (father-in-law). Firm: Strickland, Blodgett and Law (1920–1932). Designed high-style hotels (the Ritz-Carlton), apartments, stores, and residences. The firm continued under his son Charles, who specialized in Colonial restorations and style. D22.

SYMMES, MAINI AND MC KEE. General architects and engineers. C26.

UPJOHN, RICHARD (1802–1878). English-born, Upjohn reflected the English Gothic Revival influence of A. W. N. Pugin in church and residential designs. A founder of the American Institute of Architects, he served as its first president. A7.

VAN BRUNT, HENRY (1832–1903). Harvard. Apprenticeship: George Snell, Richard M. Hunt. Firm: Ware and Van Brunt. A founder of the American Institute of Architects and Boston Society of Architects, Van Brunt synthesized a variety of nineteenth-century styles in Harvard's Memorial Hall (1865–78), Wellesley College's Billings Hall, and as a designer of the World Columbian Exposition. A11.

VINAL, ARTHUR (active 1876–1921). Apprenticeship: office of Peabody and Stearns. Broad range of building types in collaboration with his brother, a speculator/builder, and as City Architect (1884–85). Vinal's good taste makes a solid contribution to his Bay State Road townhouses. B31, C5, D5, D6, D7b, D11.

VON STORCH. Firms: Von Storch and Burkavage, Von Storch and Steffian. C4, C31.

WARE, WILLIAM R. (1832–1915). Lawrence Scientific School (Harvard). Apprenticeship: Cabot, Richard M. Hunt. Firm: Ware and Van Brunt. Founder of modern architectural education in U.S. First Professor of Architecture at M.I.T. (1866) and Columbia (1881). Peabody and Stearns trained in his office. A11.

WARNECKE, JOHN CARL. C10, D33.

WETHERELL, GEORGE H. (1854–1930). M.I.T., Ecole des Beaux-Arts. Apprenticeship: Nathaniel L. Bradlee, leading Boston architect. Firm: Winslow, Wetherall and Bigelow. After the Great Boston Fire of 1873 and into the twentieth century, the firm designed a large number of commercial buildings serving a prominent clientele. D18a, D18b.

WHARTON, EDITH (1862–1937). Famous author and tastemaker. As one of the first interior decorators, she preached that architecture and design reflected and influenced not only style of living but personality and thus, identity. See CODMAN.

WHEELWRIGHT, EDMUND M. (1854–1912). Harvard, M.I.T., Ecole des Beaux-Arts. Apprenticeship: Peabody and Stearns; McKim, Mead and White. Firm: Wheelwright and Haven. As City Architect (1891–95, more than 100 buildings), he set standards for municipal and civic buildings: New England Conservatory of Music, Massachusetts Historical Society, and (as consultant) Museum of Fine Arts, as well as the residences of the socially prominent. His boathouses, Pine Street fire tower, and the Lampoon Building (his last, in 1909) are among Boston's wittiest creations. D13, D28; pp. 8, 118.

WILCOX, FRANK. Speculator apartment builder. D2.

WINSLOW, WALTER T. (1843–1909). Paris. Apprenticeship: Nathaniel Bradlee. Firm: Winslow, Wetherell and Bigelow. Commercial, public, and residential commissions. B5, D18a, D18b.

# Index of Building Types by Original Purpose

# Glossary of Architectural Styles

(Interiors are not indexed.)

ADAMESQUE. (1780–1829) The dominant American FEDERAL style which adopted the designs of the Scottish Adam brothers (1760–80). The Adams modified the existing Renaissance and Palladian styles which were based upon Greek and Roman public architecture. They combined the elegant, planar, balanced proportions and vocabulary of domestic Classical Roman homes and palaces with delicate French rococo motifs. Flexible interior plan introduce new geometric shapes: oval, circular, and hexagonal.

ART DECO. (1925–40) A style of decoration used primarily in public buildings to create a dramatic, futuristic effect through the use of stylized, hard-edged, angular, shallow (sometimes recessed) patterns in combination with stone, metal, or terra-cotta. The building mass steps back from a broad base to the narrower top, increasing the sense of verticality.

BEAUX ARTS. See CLASSICAL REVIVAL.

CLASSICAL REVIVAL. A term evoking the vocabulary, balanced proportions, and smooth surfaces of ancient Greek and Roman buildings.

> BEAUX ARTS. (1888–1950) The philosophy of the Ecole des Beaux-Arts, which emphasized French seventeenth-century monumentality, symmetry, and rational axial planning. It is found primarily in public buildings and mansions.

> FRENCH CLASSICAL REVIVAL. A domestic style based upon seventeenth-

century French models, in which a sense of harmony prevails. Colors are subdued and light in tone. Elegant, symmetrical panels, slightly embellished with rococo trim, are frequently employed on walls and fireplace surrounds.

> CLASSICAL GREEK REVIVAL. A decorative vocabulary, such as anthemion leaf, Greek key, square windows with cross mullions, and heavy double doors that is sometimes applied to classical exteriors.

COLLEGIATE GOTHIC. See GOTHIC REVIVAL.

COLONIAL REVIVAL. (1870–1920) Domestic architecture that employs a variety of eighteenth-century motifs and materials but in an eclectic combination and, generally, exaggerated symmetrical proportions. As an indigenous style, it dominated New England building, often incorporating authentic fragments. Forms include:

> FEDERAL REVIVAL. (1890–1940) Influenced by ADAMESQUE and French rationalist examples, facades feature taut surfaces, symmetrical fenestration (diminishing in size), bow fronts, elliptical fanlights, and, inside, oval rooms and curved staircases.

> GEORGIAN REVIVAL. (1890–1915) A form of Colonial Revival which utilizes rich, robust, sculptural English Georgian (1740–1780) Classical columns, cornices, corner pilasters, quoins, and carved ornamentation within a symmetrical rectangular shape and hipped roof. Interiors ex-

hibit heavy carved wood and plaster plant and geometric forms on moldings and ceilings. The Revival form, however, increased the scale and combination of elements into a richer, eclectic presence.

CONTEMPORARY. (1946–to date) Styles that emphasize manmade materials (metal, concrete, glass, and enameled surfaces). Manipulation of geometric forms and fenestration creates a powerful presence, devoid of historical references.

FEDERAL REVIVAL. See COLONIAL REVIVAL.

FRENCH CLASSICAL REVIVAL. See CLASSICAL REVIVAL.

GEORGIAN REVIVAL. See COLONIAL REVIVAL.

GOTHIC REVIVAL. (1830–1930) The style recreated a medieval age of pageantry and handicraft which, however, emphasized different aspects in succeeding decades.

> EARLY GOTHIC REVIVAL. (1840s) First appeared in America in church architecture imitating English forms. By 1840, it had become popular for suburban domestic structures. These featured steep roofs, clustered chimneys, and asymmetrical composition, set in a picturesque "natural landscape."

> HIGH VICTORIAN GOTHIC. (1850–75) The popular choice for mid-century church and public buildings. These strong, assymmetrical shapes often reflected the theories of the Englishman John Ruskin, who advocated multicolored stones (polychromy), foliated forms, pointed-arch windows, and dramatic spires.

> LATE GOTHIC REVIVAL. (1895–1940) A style widely espoused by R. A. Cram for church and public buildings. It derives from the PERPENDICULAR LATE GOTHIC style employing flat arched windows, smoother stone facades, and, often, beautifully carved ornament; known also as COLLEGIATE GOTHIC.

TUDOR REVIVAL. (1895–1940) An imitation of late-sixteenth-century Elizabethan domestic form in brick with stone details, rectangular windows, and tall clustered chimneys. It is often combined with Jacobean (Jacobethan) details such as strapwork. The style was so prevalent in the 1920s that it was known as Stockbroker Tudor.

GREEK REVIVAL. (1820–1860) This style became a tribute to the ideals of Greek democracy as the young United States enthusiastically adopted the white (marble-like) rectangular temple form with a low-pitched gable roof. Its columns and strong simple moldings conform to designs of the Classical Orders.

INTERNATIONAL. (1920–1945) A product of machine-age engineering and materials (concrete, steel, and glass) produced a stark skeletal frame sheathed with a smooth, uniform wall surface and ribbon windows. Box-like and unornamented, the style could be applied cosmetically to renovations of existing facades. The flexible, open interior plan serves equally for public, commercial, and domestic functions.

ITALIAN RENAISSANCE REVIVAL. (1850–1875) Inspired by the Roman Coliseum, with its wide arches, superimposed Classical Orders, and bold cornices. This richly sculptural style was a perfect complement to mass-produced cast iron-building facades of the post–Civil War economic boon.

ITALIANATE. (1840–1880) An extremely popular box-like, two- or three-story symmetrical house style with tall rectangular windows (sometimes paired), polygonal bays, central porch, and wide overhanging eaves supported by brackets. Moldings, rusticated quoins, and the central porch produce a formal effect.

MISSION REVIVAL. (1890–1920) A reinterpretation of the American West's "Spanish Colonial Revival." Based upon seventeenth-century Catholic missions, its Mediterranean origins appear in tile roofs, smooth white plaster or stuccoed walls, and bold curved arches. The emphasis upon simplicity and "authentic" materials allied the style with the Arts and Crafts movement.

NEO-CLASSICAL. (1780–1860) A style dependent upon classical Greek and Roman vocabulary, elegant geometric forms, and symmetry. It spanned periods from Adam through the Greek Revival.

NEO-GREC. (1870–80) A popular type of ornament composed of flat, machine-incised patterns of stylized classical fluting, plant forms, and geometric designs; adopted from the French.

PERPENDICULAR GOTHIC. See GOTHIC REVIVAL.

QUEEN ANNE REVIVAL. (1876–1900) A highly individual and picturesque style which combined classical motifs and medieval forms in a bewildering variety of materials, textures, colors, roofs, gables, windows, and shapes. Of English origin, this inventive, assymmetrical design suited a rich United States, one searching back for its seventeenth-century roots but with new wealth and the evolving technology to assemble such buildings.

RENAISSANCE REVIVAL. (1840–1890) A re-minder of sixteenth-century Italian High Renaissance palaces, creating a dignified, formal effect. Classical, architrave-framed windows and rusticated-quoin detail accent the symmetrical, smooth, ashlar stone facades.

ROMANESQUE (RICHARDSONIAN) REVIVAL. (1870–1900) An indigenous American style translated by H. H. Richardson from European Romanesque–style buildings. Bold arches, rough-cut stone, deep openings, ribbon-like windows, and broad roof planes integrate the heavy, horizontal mass to create a sense of solidity. The ornament of carved and molded foliate forms lightens the lithic, almost geologic, nature of the structures.

SECOND EMPIRE. (1860–1890) Imitates the version of the seventeenth-century Classical style adopted by Emperor Napoleon III in his reconstruction of Paris. Second Empire style is similar to the Italianate in its symmetrical, rectangular composition. Distinguishing features include the high mansard roof resting on a prominent cornice, and, on high-style and public buildings, projecting pavilions with lavish, three-dimensional Classical motifs.

TUDOR REVIVAL. See GOTHIC REVIVAL.

# Glossary of Architectural Terms

ACANTHUS LEAF. Thistle-like, scalloped leaf form used as ornament on classical Corinthian and Composite capitals.

ACROTERIUM. Carved decorative feature, usually on a pedestal at the apex and lower ends of a pediment or along the roofline.

ADAPTIVE REUSE. The renovation of a building into a new use.

APRON. The horizontal panel below a window sill. See SPANDREL.

ARCADE. A row of arches supported on piers or columns, sometimes supporting a covered passage.

ASHLAR. Building stones hewn or dressed to a carefully squared, smooth face, laid with thin joints.

ATRIUM. The inner court of a Roman house, open to the sky and surrounded by the roof.

BALUSTER/BANISTER/SPINDLE. A short post, often urn-shaped, supporting a rail and used in a series to form a BALUSTRADE.

BALUSTRADE. See BALUSTER.

BAY. Vertical divisions, such as windows and doors. Building elevation is frequently measured by bays.

BAY WINDOW. A polygonal or semicircular window element projecting from a wall at ground level and continuing up one or more stories; an ORIEL WINDOW if projecting from the upper floor only; a BOW WINDOW if curved; a BOWFRONT if a dominant element in the facade.

BELT COURSE/BELT CORNICE. See STRINGCOURSE.

BLIND ARCH/RECESSED ARCH. An arch-shaped recess in a wall that has no actual window opening.

BOLECTION MOLDING. A heavy, projecting curved molding usually covering the joint between different surface levels.

BOND. ENGLISH when bricks are laid in alternate COURSES of stretchers (long side) and headers (short end) to the weather. FLEMISH where a single brick course is laid with alternating stretchers (long side) and headers (short end) facing the weather.

BOWFRONT. See BAY WINDOW.

BRACKET. A small member supporting an overhang and projecting from the face of a wall, frequently used for decoration.

BRISE DE SOLEIL. A free-standing or attached grille of vertical and horizontal fins used to screen the sun from a contemporary-style window facade.

BROKEN PEDIMENT. See PEDIMENT.

BUTTRESS. A short section of wall built at right angles to one of the main outer walls of a building to give additional strength at a pressure point.

CANTED. Inclined, having sloping sides.

CAPITAL. The moldings and carved enrichment at the top of a column, pilaster, or pier, which supports an entablature.

CARTOUCHE. Ornament in the form of elaborate scrolled forms around shields, often bearing an insignia or motto.

CARYATID. Sculptured figure used as a support or column.

CLASSICAL ORDER. See ORDER.

182

CLERESTORY. That part of a building which rises above the roof of another part and which has windows in its walls; also, the upper stage of the main walls of a church, pierced by windows.

CLOISTER. An arcade in an ecclesiastical setting.

COFFER. A recessed panel, usually square or octagonal, in a ceiling or underside of a classical arch.

COLONNADE. A row of connected columns.

COLOSSAL/GIANT ORDER. See Giant Colossal Order.

CONSOLE. A projecting, vertical scroll-shaped member at least twice as high as deep, used as a bracket or corbel.

CORBEL. A carved stone block or successive courses of blocks supporting a beam or other horizontal member.

CORINTHIAN. An elaborate late-Greek and Roman classical order whose capitals are embellished with acanthus and curved fern-leaf motifs.

CORNICE. The crowning, projecting member of a classical entablature or building.

COURSE. A row of building blocks (bricks or stones) extending the full length and thickness of a wall.

CRENELLATION. A fortress-like parapet of alternating indentations and raised portions.

CRESTING. An ornamental finish along the top of a roof, wall, or screen, usually decorated and sometimes perforated.

CROCKET. One of a series of projecting, evenly spaced, leaf-like knobs which ornament the outside surface of gables, pinnacles, or spires.

CROSS-GABLE. Two double-pitched roofs which meet at right angles. See also GABLE.

CUL-DE-SAC. A dead-end street, sometimes with a turnaround.

CUPOLA. A small, domed, lantern-like structure crowning a roof or turret, usu-

ally for ornamental purposes.

DENTIL MOLDING. An ornamental series of small tooth-like blocks used in classical orders.

DORIC. The simplest classical order, featuring unadorned columns supporting a frieze of fluted triglyphs alternating with plain panels or metopes.

ECOLE DES BEAUX-ARTS. A rigorous system of French architectural training dating from the seventeenth century, stressing rational, axial plans within a classical vocabulary. By the 1870s, it had become a powerful influence for professional architects worldwide.

ENFILADE. The alignment of all doors between the rooms in a series so as to produce a vista.

ENGAGED (APPLIED) COLUMN. A classical column attached or embedded within a wall, projecting less than three-fourths of its circumference.

ENTABLATURE. All the top horizontal portion of a classical order between the column capital and roof, consisting of a lower architrave, frieze, and upper cornice.

FACADE. An elevation or exterior of a building, usually the principal front.

FINIAL. An ornament, usually a knob or foliate form, at the apex of an architectural feature such as a roof, pinnacle, etc.

FIREPLACE FACING. The finish veneer, such as marble or carvings, covering the rough construction around the firebox.

FLUTING. Parallel, shallow, concave, vertical carved grooves in the shaft of a column, pilaster, or other surface.

FRENCH DOORS/WINDOWS. Floor-length windows which open like a book.

FRENCH FLAT. Term used in Boston in the 1850s when the first apartment buildings were introduced from Paris.

FRESCO. A wall mural which is painted directly onto fresh wet plaster.

FRIEZE. The middle and most ornamented part of a classical entablature.

GABLE. The triangular, sometimes curved, upper portion of wall closing the end of a double-pitched roof.

GAMBREL. A roof with two slopes of different pitch on either side of the ridge; an eighteenth-century form similar to mansard.

GIANT (COLOSSAL) ORDER. A late-classical order where columns rise from the ground two or more stories.

GREEK RUNNING KEY/GREEK FRET. A continuous motif of interlocking rectangular patterns.

GUILLOCHE (running). A pattern of curved, interlacing bands forming a braid-like molding enrichment.

GUTTAE. Conical shapes carved onto the mutules of a Doric entablature.

HALF-TIMBER. A technique combining medieval wooden frame and infill construction in which the members are exposed on the outside wall. In a Revival form, MOCK HALF TIMBERS are placed upon a finished wall.

HEADER. A brick laid with its short face to the weather.

HIPPED ROOF. A roof with slopes on all four walls.

HISTORIC DISTRICTS—1. NATIONAL REGISTER. A collection of buildings, structures, sites, subjects, and spaces that possess integrity of location, design, setting, materials, workmanship, feeling, and association. This designation provides benefits and protection.
—2. LOCAL. A district in which a design review is required for any alterations visible from the public way.

HOOD MOLDING. A miniature roof supported by brackets projecting over a doorway window to deflect rain.

IN ANTIS. Columns set within a recess rather than set out as a porch.

INGLENOOK. A seat built at right angles to a fireplace. The hearth was important in the Queen Anne period as a symbol of the center of the home.

IONIC. A simple classical order; its capital resembles a double scroll (the two parts of which are called volutes).

JERKINHEAD DORMER. A three-sided gable roof truncated above the front section.

KEYSTONE. The central, wedge-shaped stone at the crown of an arch; also BROKEN KEYSTONE.

LINTEL. A weight-bearing horizontal stone slab, timber, or steel beam spanning an opening and supported on columns or walls.

LIVING HALL. A medieval-inspired oversized central hall, usually with fireplace, which served as a gathering place, the heart of an English Queen Anne Revival–style home.

LOW RELIEF. Carved or cast designs raised from or attached to a background panel.

MANSARD. A double roof with two slopes to all four sides, the lower one being much steeper than the upper and acting as a wall. It is a misspelling of the name of the architect François Mansart (1598–1666) inventor of such roofs, which were revived in Paris during the Second Empire (1852–70) of Napoleon III.

MEDALLION. A round or oval sculpted plain or carved panel.

METOPE. The space between the triglyphs of a Doric frieze, often decorated with carved ornament.

MODILLION. A small ornamental bracket of the Corinthian or Composite order usually found in a series supporting a projecting molding or cornice.

MODULAR DESIGN. A system of design using materials fabricated from repeated, interchangeable sections.

MODULOR. A system of proportions advocated by Le Corbusier (1951) based upon the human figure and used to determine proportions of buildings.

MOLDING. A strip of curvilinear profile projecting from a surface.

MULLION. A vertical bar dividing a window into two or more units, or dividing a wall opening into two or more windows.

MUTULE. The projecting square blocks above the triglyph and on the soffit (underside) of Doric cornices, from which the guttae suspend.

"NATURAL LANDSCAPE." The eighteenth-century English country-estate designs of smooth rolling hills punctuated by carefully placed trees advocated by Capability Brown.

NAVE. The main body of a church from the entrance to the chancel.

NEWEL POST. The principal post at the end of a flight of stairs.

ORDER (CLASSICAL). A decorative and proportional post-and-lintel system, five of which were developed by the Greeks and Romans.

ORIEL WINDOW. See BAY WINDOW.

ORMOLU. Ornamental bronze or brass, cast, then chiseled by hand and gilded with gold leaf or, later, lacquer.

OVERHANG. A system of timber construction in the fifteenth century in which the upper story is thrust out over the lower on joists and/or a curved brace.

OVERMANTEL. The paneling in decorative motifs forming the upper part of a fireplace enframement.

PALLADIAN. Correct, elegant, and studied classical vocabulary, based upon the Venetian Renaissance designs of Andrea Palladio, which dominated English style from c. 1720 to 1760.

PALLADIAN/VENETIAN/SERLIANA. A round-headed central section flanked by lower square-headed windows, all of which are separated by columns or pilasters.

PARAPET. A low wall, solid or perforated, at the edge of a roof, balcony, etc, sometimes formed by an extension of the wall below.

PARTY WALL. A structural interior wall, shared by but dividing two vertical row-houses.

PAVILION. A wing or central unit which projects from a larger architectural unit and extends to the roofline. It is usually accented by special decorative treatment.

PEDIMENT. A low, triangular Classical gable formed by the roof slopes on top and cornice beneath, supported on the entablature over porticoes, windows, and doors. When the slopes return before reaching the apex it is BROKEN (or open).

PENDANT. A fixed, hanging ornament, usually the projecting lower end of a part of the construction.

PIANO NOBILE. The principal and tallest floor in a classical building containing the reception rooms.

PICTURESQUE. An early-nineteenth-century Romantic esthetic evoking rugged nature. Applied in architecture through siting, asymmetry, and a variety of materials and textures.

PILASTER. A simple, rectilinear projection of a wall which serves as an attached column. The cap and base are treated as a free-standing column and conform to Classical orders.

PLAT. A ground or plot plan or map.

PLINTH. A pedestal, usually square in section, supporting a column or sculpture.

POCKET DOOR. A paneled door which slides in and out of a box built within a wall. Usually found as a pair that opens up two rooms "enfilade" into one space.

POINT (MORTAR). To finish off the joints with decorative modeling of a superior mortar.

POLYCHROMY. The use of colored building materials to articulate sections of a building and for ornamentation. Strongly recommended by John Ruskin, it was typical of the High-Victorian Gothic style.

PORTE-COCHERE. Used in the United States to describe a porch large enough for a wheeled vehicle to pass through.

PORTICO. An entrance porch consisting

of a low-pitched pedimented roof supported on classical columns.

POST. An upright piece; a pillar.

PRESSED METAL. The result of an inexpensive process whereby metal sheathing is stamped to imitate elaborate decorative moldings or carvings.

PYLON. A tall, Egyptian, pyramidal ceremonial post or finial typical of the Elizabethan and Jacobean periods.

QUARRY-FACED. The natural, rough state of stone after it is split at the quarry; rugged.

QUARRY/QUARREL-GLASS. Small, usually diagonally-placed panes of glass set in lead strips.

QUARTER GRAIN. Four slices of wood veneer opened out to form a circular pattern.

QUOIN. Dressed stones ornamenting a building, usually prominent, with faces laid to alternate large and small; from the French *coin* or corner.

RAMP RAIL. A concave, connecting sweep in a vertical stair rail where it turns at a horizontal landing.

RECESSED ARCH. See BLIND ARCH.

RISER. The vertical portion of a stairstep which supports the horizontal tread.

ROCOCO. The final, elaborate, light, and delicately scaled stage of the Baroque style characterized by double-curved and shell forms.

ROSETTE. A flat, stylized, circular or oval shape used as a decorative floral medallion.

ROUGH-AGGREGATE. Poured concrete mixed with pebbles which produces a Contemporary-style textured wall surface.

RUSTICATED. A kind of masonry, usually roughened, with a beveled edge, set with deep joints to imitate Classical structures.

SASH. A window frame of glass panes that slides up and down vertically. The sash is described by the number of panes

in it: for example, nine over six refers to nine panes in the upper sash and six in the lower. Imported from Holland to England in the late-seventeenth century.

SOFFIT. The underside of any limited architectural element such as a lintel or arch.

SPANDREL. 1. The surface between two arches. 2. The wall or panel immediately below a window, often treated in a decorative manner such as an apron.

SPECULATOR. An investor or builder who constructs a building at his/her own expense, planning to attract an unknown buyer.

SPINDLE. See BALUSTER.

SPLAT. The broad, central member of a chair back or side.

SPLAYED. Pertaining to a sloping, chamfered surface cut into walls. Usually refers to the widening of wall openings by slanting the sides.

STOCK. A mass-produced item purchased by a builder in contrast to a custom-designed feature.

STRAPWORK. A Jacobean-period form of ornament using lines of decoration or flat, leather-like straps with raised edges which are intertwined to form panels.

STRETCHER. A brick laid with its long face to the weather.

STRIATED. Pertaining to a shallow, mechanically-incised fluting characteristic of the Neo-Grec style.

STRINGCOURSE. A narrow projecting horizontal band across the wall of a building, at any level.

SWAN'S NECK PEDIMENT. A broken pediment where the top moldings terminate in a curving, swan-neck shape.

TABBED HOOD. A Gothic-Revival window surround with short, horizontal ears.

TAPESTRY BRICK. Colored bricks laid to give the effect of woven patterns, an Arts and Crafts form imitating primitive cultures.

186

TERRA-COTTA. Fine-grained reddish-brown clay building blocks fired in molds of intricately detailed patterns.

TERRAZZO. A flooring finish of marble chips mixed with cement mortar and laid *in situ*; the surface is then ground and polished.

TRACERY. Ornamental bands or curves of stone or lead ornamenting a window or transom/fanlight into which glass is set.

TRANSOM. A narrow, horizontal window unit over a door; a curved transom is known as a fanlight.

TREFOIL/QUATREFOIL. A decorative three- or four-leaf shape found in Gothic window tracery and paneling.

TRIGLYPH. A fluted block which separates the metopes in a Doric frieze.

TRUSS. A large, rigid, open, triangular framework made up of braces, struts, and ties and used to span large spaces.

VERDIGRISED COPPER. A green patina formed on copper by oxidation.

VERGEBOARD/BARGEBOARD. The facing-board, sawn or carved in Gothic-Revival motifs, attached to the incline of a gable.

VERNACULAR. Everyday, in contrast to important public styles of structures; folk-like.

VOLUTE. The scroll or spiral ornamenting Ionic and later-classical capitals.

WAINSCOT/WAINSCOTING. Wood paneling, usually covering the lower half of a wall; erroneously called a dado.

WATERSTRUCK BRICK. A brick with a hard, smooth finish produced by lining the brick mold with water rather than sand.